Frank Lloyd Wright

The People to Know Series

Neil Armstrong
*The First Man
on the Moon*
0-89490-828-6

Isaac Asimov
Master of Science Fiction
0-7660-1031-7

Bill Clinton
United States President
0-89490-437-X

Hillary Rodham Clinton
Activist First Lady
0-89490-583-X

Bill Cosby
Actor and Comedian
0-89490-548-1

Willa Cather
Writer of the Prairie
0-89490-980-0

Walt Disney
Creator of Mickey Mouse
0-89490-694-1

Bob Dole
Legendary Senator
0-89490-825-1

Marian Wright Edelman
*Fighting for
Children's Rights*
0-89490-623-2

Bill Gates
*Billionaire
Computer Genius*
0-89490-824-3

Jane Goodall
*Protector of
Chimpanzees*
0-89490-827-8

Al Gore
*United States
Vice President*
0-89490-496-5

Tipper Gore
*Activist, Author,
Photographer*
0-7660-1142-9

Ernest Hemingway
Writer and Adventurer
0-89490-979-7

Ron Howard
*Child Star &
Hollywood Director*
0-89490-981-9

John F. Kennedy
*President of the
New Frontier*
0-89490-693-3

John Lennon
*The Beatles
and Beyond*
0-89490-702-6

Jack London
*A Writer's
Adventurous Life*
0-7660-1144-5

Maya Lin
Architect and Artist
0-89490-499-X

Barbara McClintock
*Nobel Prize
Geneticist*
0-89490-983-5

Christopher Reeve
*Hollywood's Man
of Courage*
0-7660-1149-6

Ann Richards
*Politician, Feminist,
Survivor*
0-89490-497-3

Sally Ride
*First American Woman
in Space*
0-89490-829-4

Will Rogers
Cowboy Philosopher
0-89490-695-X

Franklin D. Roosevelt
*The Four-Term
President*
0-89490-696-8

Steven Spielberg
*Hollywood
Filmmaker*
0-89490-697-6

Martha Stewart
*Successful
Businesswoman*
0-89490-984-3

Amy Tan
*Author of
The Joy Luck Club*
0-89490-699-2

Alice Walker
*Author of
The Color Purple*
0-89490-620-8

Simon Wiesenthal
*Tracking Down
Nazi Criminals*
0-89490-830-8

Frank Lloyd Wright
Visionary Architect
0-7660-1032-5

People to Know

Frank Lloyd Wright
Visionary Architect

David K. Wright

Enslow Publishers, Inc.
44 Fadem Road   PO Box 38
Box 699   Aldershot
Springfield, NJ 07081 Hants GU12 6BP
USA   UK
http://www.enslow.com

J B WRIGHT

Publisher's Note: *Frank Lloyd Wright changed some facts in his autobiography, and in other sources dates and facts vary. The publisher would like to thank Jack Holzhueter of the State Historical Society of Wisconsin for his assistance.*

Library of Congress Cataloging-in-Publication Data

Wright, David K.
    Frank Lloyd Wright : visionary architect / David K. Wright.
        p. cm. — (People to know)
    Includes bibliographical references and index.
    Summary: Examines the life and career of the American architect, detailing the evolution of his innovative design and the structures which won him fame around the world.
    ISBN 0-7660-1032-5
    1. Wright, Frank Lloyd, 1867–1959—Juvenile literature.
    2. Architects—United States—Biography—Juvenile literature.
    [1. Wright, Frank Lloyd, 1867–1959. 2. Architects.] I. Title.
    II. Series.
    NA737.W7W67   1998
    720'.92—dc21
    [B]
                                                97-29056
                                                CIP
                                                    AC
Printed in the United States of America

10 9 8 7 6 5 4 3 2 1

To Our Readers:
All Internet addresses in this book were active and appropriate when we went to press. Any comments or suggestions can be sent by e-mail to Comments@enslow.com or to the address on the back cover.

Contents

Frank Lloyd Wright

Witness to Tragedy

In 1883, Frank Lloyd Wright was a sixteen-year-old high school student with a lot on his mind. Somewhat of a misfit, he was nervous around girls and impatient with most of the boys in his classes. Frank wanted to be an architect—a designer of buildings. He had known for some time what he planned to do with his life, and he was eager to get on with it. Young Wright often ambled through the downtown streets of Madison, Wisconsin, studying the architecture of the city buildings. A few blocks from his school, two new wings were being added to the massive State Capitol Building. The sounds of construction echoed through the streets.

The 1880s were exciting years to be an American,

for Frank and for everyone else. The Civil War had been over for nearly twenty years, railroads now stretched from one coast to the other, and telephones and electric lights were coming into greater and greater use. The Statue of Liberty was under construction in New York's harbor. In Chicago, there remained a great deal of rebuilding to be done after the huge, disastrous fire that had swept through the city in 1871.

At 1:40 P.M. on November 8, 1883, a thunderous roar suddenly shook the city of Madison.[1] Later, Wright would describe how the new south wing of the capitol, still under construction, collapsed before his very eyes. Stunned like those around him, Frank peered over the fence surrounding the building site.[2] As the dust settled, he was horrified to see mangled construction workers amid the clutter of broken stone. Several men ran blindly from the building site as others screamed in agony. Still others did not move.

The dust cloud from the accident hung above the capitol dome during frantic attempts at rescue. Huge pieces of stone continued to crumble into the basement. The brand-new wing was now a vast pile of rubble. Firefighters arrived but were warned to beware of further collapse. They were unable to lift the huge chunks of sandstone and the massive iron beams. So they dug frantically into the piles with shovels and with their hands, often too late to free a victim. Frank continued to hang on to the fence, stunned. He had never before seen any human tragedy, and this would leave its mark on him for the rest of his life.[3] His sorrow intensified after the arrival of the workers' wives. Their cries could be heard above the shouts of the firefighters and the clatter of passing wagons.

Frank was, he later recalled, "heartsick" over the tragedy in which eight men died.[4] He learned that the accident need not have happened. Huge concrete piers in the basement, designed to support hundreds of tons—the full weight of the building—had collapsed. The failure of these piers meant that all the floors and interior walls failed, too.

The building's architect had designed the piers well. But the contractors saw their size and decided to save money by filling them with broken bricks and other rubble rather than with solid concrete.

The architect, a competent professional, was charged with manslaughter and found guilty. He never designed another building. He was "tried by a jury of his peers and condemned," Frank Lloyd Wright wrote years later.[5] The young student could not put the bloody scene out of his mind. He had terrible dreams for several nights afterward, and he became depressed.[6]

Also around this time, Frank's parents divorced, adding to his unhappiness. Frank did not give up his goal of becoming an architect, but he soon lost patience with high school, quitting before he graduated. Although he lacked a high school diploma, he was later admitted to the University of Wisconsin, a couple of miles from his home, as a special, part-time student. After only three courses in his one year there, he realized that college was not meeting his needs. The school did not offer classes in architecture, so Frank took basic engineering instead.

Wright was also trying to pursue his career interest. One of the engineering professors, Allan D. Conover, gave him a part-time job as a draftsman for $35 a month. Wright attended class in the morning, worked in the afternoon, and studied in the evening. Still, drafting and calculating and memorizing had little to do with his real dream of designing dramatic homes and big buildings. Again he quit school, determined to seek his fortune in Chicago, one hundred fifty miles southeast. He would look for an architectural firm that wanted a bright and ambitious employee.

To finance the train ride to the Windy City, Wright sold a couple of expensive books that had belonged to his father. He was paid a few dollars for a genuine fur collar his loving mother had sewn to his winter coat. After buying a one-way ticket, Frank stepped onto the departing train with a bag of clothing and just seven dollars in his pocket. He also brought along a few drawings, to show his architectural and drawing skills.

Hundreds of building ideas rattled around in his head as the train chugged through the Midwest farmland. The tragedy of the State Capitol wreckage had also made a lifelong impression.[7] Frank Lloyd Wright never forgot the lesson he learned about building materials and safety in construction.

"A Prophetic Birth"

Frank Lincoln Wright was born on June 8, 1867, in Richland Center, Wisconsin. (He later changed his middle name to Lloyd.) There were already three children in the house, though Frank was his mother's first child. Anna Lloyd Jones, Frank's mother, had married William Russell Cary Wright after the death of Wright's first wife. Anna became the stepmother of his two boys and a girl. Although the couple had two more children after Frank—Jane, born in 1869, and Maginel, born in 1877—no other child was Frank's equal in his mother's eyes.[1]

"Yours was a prophetic birth," she once said to him. Frank evidently liked that idea. A captivating speaker and writer, Wright later told people that

Frank Lloyd Wright as a young boy. Even before her son was born, Wright's mother planned his future as a great architect. "I was born an architect," he later said.

lightning had ignited the clouds and trees had swayed in a mighty wind as a magnificent late-spring storm announced his arrival.[2]

Anna Lloyd Jones, at twenty-eight, was about fourteen years younger than her husband when they married. Frank's father was a teacher, a musician, and a Baptist minister. His mother was a teacher. She filled Frank's head with history and legends about Wales as soon as he seemed able to hear her voice. She had been born in Wales, the windswept, mountainous western edge of Great Britain. The stories often involved mystical Druids, the ancient Welsh priests who were said to be magicians or wizards. She explained that there was a special link between the Welsh and the great outdoors. Frank grew up having a strong appreciation for nature.[3]

Frank loved his mother and respected his father.[4] William Wright tried his hand at a lot of things, such as law and medicine, and most did not go well financially. He enjoyed the ministry, and he spent long hours composing music. His most lasting impression on young Frank may have been the passionate music of Beethoven. William Wright played Beethoven constantly on the family piano and tried to compose equally moving sonatas. Years later, in his autobiography, Frank Lloyd Wright recalled his father, ink staining his face from a pen clenched in his teeth, slaving over just the right notes for a musical composition.[5]

William Wright was constantly on the lookout for financial opportunity, and the family moved often. Between 1869 and 1873, they lived in McGregor,

Iowa; Spring Green, Wisconsin; and Pawtucket, Rhode Island. In 1874, when Frank was seven, the family moved to Weymouth, Massachusetts. Once in the Boston area, Wright tried to revive a Baptist congregation whose church had burned. The local newspaper praised his work, but in the end he failed.

Besides not being able to tell good opportunities from bad, William Wright was often in need of money.[6] So the family was fortunate to be able to take one brief vacation in 1876 to attend the Centennial Exposition in Philadelphia, several hundred miles from their home in Massachusetts.

Frank's mother had given up her teaching career when she married, but she remained vitally interested in the education of small children. She especially admired the ideas of an outstanding German educator named Friedrich Froebel. Froebel believed that children should learn naturally rather than be drilled by teachers in classrooms. He devised simple learning games, called "gifts," that would stir a child's imagination. While at the Centennial Exposition, Anna Wright bought Frank a set of Froebel's "gift" blocks in various shapes. He played with them endlessly, building tiny structures with the cubes, spheres, triangles, and other shapes. The blocks and geometric shapes played a major role in helping to develop his talents as an architect. Wright later wrote that "the smooth cardboard triangles and maplewood blocks were most important. All are in my fingers to this day."[7]

The family returned to Wisconsin in 1878, moving into a very modest home in downtown Madison. Anna

A set of Froebel blocks helped ignite Frank's creativity when he was a child. The blocks came with instructions for learning games, called "gifts."

Wright had many brothers and sisters, and they helped support the family while William Wright made a meager living teaching music. One brother brought the Wright family a cow from forty miles away in Spring Green so the children would have fresh milk to drink. The animal shared space in the backyard with a chicken coop. About the same time, Frank's mother arranged for him to spend his summers working on the farm of one of her brothers in Spring Green. Frank was eleven years old.

Frank loved his Uncle James Lloyd Jones, but at the beginning he disliked farm life.[8] First of all, it seemed as if it started just a few minutes after he went to bed each evening. Frank slept upstairs, and when it was time to wake up, his uncle banged on the stovepipe that ran up the wall past Frank's bed. Uncle James and Aunt Laura got up at 4:00 A.M. every day. Frank pulled on work clothing and ate a quick break- fast before heading to the barn to help milk the cows. This kind of work was new to him, but he soon learned.

Frank stacked cords of wood, fed the calves, split oak rails for fencing, and did dozens of other chores. Often Frank seemed to have run out of energy but still had to finish the day's work. Before long he began to understand the Lloyd Jones family's motto, " . . . to add 'tired' to 'tired' and add it again—and add it yet again."[9] His only break came with a bath each Saturday night and church on Sunday morning. His mother paid him a visit in midsummer and cried when she saw that his hands were rough and his clothes ragged.[10]

Mrs. Wright also knew the dangers a young farmhand might face. On one sunny afternoon, as crops were being harvested, Frank ran barefoot to the water jug at the edge of a field. He took a long drink, set the jug down—and found himself eye-to-eye with a rattlesnake. The boy held still for a moment, then quickly grabbed a pitchfork. He wedged the snake's head between two of the tines, then smashed it over and over with the heavy jug. His uncle scolded him for going after the snake while barefoot. Uncle James knew that the snake could easily have killed Frank with a single strike.

Frank longed for the beginning of school in the city in the fall. Despite his young age, he was resentful because he believed that farm life was wearing him out.[11] After a disagreement with his aunt because he had forgotten to return a hammer to its proper place, Frank ran away. He took a kitchen knife with him for protection, threw the hammer into a creek, and hiked off in search of a ferryboat ride across the Wisconsin River. Another uncle, Enos, found him sitting on a river dock, awaiting the ferry. Uncle Enos was sympathetic, and Frank agreed to return to the home of Uncle James and Aunt Laura. During the five summers spent on the farm, Frank ran away a few times, but he always returned.

His mother's large family had a lasting influence on Frank Lloyd Wright. These hardworking people strongly believed in science and rational thought and were Unitarians. Frank's father followed the Baptist religion, with its emphasis on personal salvation. In contrast, Unitarians emphasized the unity and harmony of all things. (Frank's father became a Unitarian when the family moved back to Wisconsin.) The members of the Lloyd Jones family defended their views with the Welsh motto "Truth against the world."[12]

What did Truth against the world mean? It meant that people like themselves might be greatly outnumbered but that if their beliefs were true, they could withstand whatever criticism might come their way. This idea was not forced on Frank. Instead, he picked it up gradually by witnessing how the large Lloyd Jones clan lived, worked, and thought. He joined them in worship on Sunday mornings, and he marveled at the preaching of a famous uncle, Jenkin Lloyd Jones. Jenkin Lloyd Jones could bring tears to the eyes of the oldest and toughest family member.

Still, it was not all serious business. Frank enjoyed getting together with his relatives. Some of the children let him lead them around, taking harmless or silly advantage of them. He once convinced young cousins that they should go home, clean up, and dress well because a party was planned later that day. When they showed up for the party, Frank's mother realized what he had done. Rather than punish him, she quickly prepared party food and drinks, saving her son from embarrassment.[13]

During summers on the farm, Frank developed what would be a lifelong love of nature. He delighted in finding birds' nests and frogs. He discovered and observed patterns in flowers and plants and came to love their colors and shapes. And he walked and walked over the land on which he would later build his home.

Back in Madison during the school year, Frank developed a friendship with a disabled boy at his school. Robie Lamp's legs were shriveled, and he walked with the aid of crutches. He and Frank took music lessons, Robie on the violin and Frank on the viola. They read a number of the same books, but their favorite plaything was a tiny printing press. Though they had little or no business, they set up their own little print shop.

Their teenage years were spent creating experiments that would lead to what they hoped would be great inventions. They lived just a block away from a lake and designed a sort of powered water boat, which they called the Frankenrob. Other inventions, such as waterwheels, bows and arrows, kites, and high-speed bobsleds, took up their time. Wright could not recall later whether any of these inventions ever worked, but he could explain in detail the ideas behind them.

In contrast, he remembered little of the time actually spent in school. Teased for his shaggy, curly hair, Frank could recall only that everyone was forced to speak in front of the class once a month. For him it was sheer torture. His grades were average, and at least once during his middle-school years, he was sent home for disciplinary reasons. He had dipped a girl's long pigtail in ink and was printing a sign with it![14] Despite such shenanigans, he appears to have learned all the basics of reading, writing, and arithmetic.

Of average height and build, Frank grew stronger with each summer spent on the farm. One day toward the end of his farm life, his uncle gave him a team of horses and told him to go by himself to work in a field. There, riding on wooden planks about the size of a garage door, Frank was to follow the horses around and around. The "planker" pulled by the horses was designed to smooth the rough dirt to make planting easier.

Farmwork can be terribly dangerous, and Frank said he felt like "a man among men" for being put in charge of the two huge horses.[15] With reins in hand, he began to ride up and down the hilly field, smoothing and reducing the size of the big clods of earth. Without warning, the planker ran over a half-hidden stump and shot forward, hitting the horses in their hind legs. The force of the moving planker caused Frank to lose his balance. He found himself hanging by the thin harness straps between the two large beasts as they ran uncontrollably up and down the field.

With every step the horses took, Frank was lifted and bounced. Yet he continued to clutch the leather straps. He knew that if he let go, he might fall beneath the planker and be badly hurt. One of his uncle's farmhands saw what was happening and ran to the field. He tried to grab the reins of one of the horses but was knocked to the ground. Luckily, his effort caused the horses to run in a big circle. The farm-hand cut them off and stopped them. Frank was covered with bruises but was not seriously hurt.

When Frank was in high school, relations between his mother and father reached a low point. Anna Wright, tired of money problems and other woes, quietly asked her husband to leave them and go his own way. He did so and they were divorced in 1885. Frank later said that he never saw his father again, though historians say this may not be true. Young Frank was convinced that his father had never loved him. In addition, the family felt shamed because divorce was considered a terrible disgrace in those days.

In 1886, Wright entered the University of Wisconsin in the civil engineering program. His family had no money to send him away to an architectural school. He was admitted to the university as a special student without having finished high school, and he was younger than many of his classmates. At university social gatherings, though he liked girls, he found himself nervous around them. Soon he began to wear the latest college styles—skintight gray pants, a graduation-style mortarboard hat with a red tassel, and fancy shoes. Over the years, Wright would be known for his distinctive clothing and his flowing hair, which was always a little longer than the current fashion.

The engineering professor for whom Wright worked as a draftsman became supervising architect for four buildings being erected at the lakeside campus. This work gave Wright the opportunity to see how buildings were constructed and to talk to the workers who were building the various structures. Among his tasks one day in the dead of winter was to check construction on a new science hall. When he discovered that part of the roof's framework was not properly secured, he climbed up a ladder and walked across slippery, ice-covered beams, several stories in the air, in order to remove the loose clips until they could be bolted correctly.

Despite such hardships, he preferred this sort of work to time spent in the classroom. Classes, he said, lacked reality. After only one year at the University of Wisconsin, Frank Lloyd Wright decided he was tired of only reading about action—he wanted to be a part of it.[16] So, at the age of nineteen, with neither a high school diploma nor a college degree, he headed for Chicago. What lay ahead for Frank Lloyd Wright in the Windy City?

The Dawn of Change

Frank Lloyd Wright did not know it, but he could hardly have chosen a better time to show up in Chicago. Nor, for that matter, could he have picked a place better suited to his temperament. The Windy City in the second half of the nineteenth century was a very energetic town, using the labor of immigrants to constantly build, improve, and expand. For example, when certain low-lying, muddy streets offended residents, enough earth was moved into Chicago to raise the streets several feet. Not everyone was well-to-do, but there was so much money being thrown around that anyone with talent had a chance to become a financial success.

Wright was aware of the ideas about architecture

that were becoming popular in Chicago. A new wave of architects and artists had grown tired of traditional, Renaissance-style buildings. The thirteenth- to sixteenth-century Renaissance, which started in Italy, had looked back to classical Greek and Roman buildings for inspiration. Traditional buildings had columns, scrollwork, cornices, and other extra decorations that some Chicago designers found useless and boring. Wright himself said that he arrived in Chicago hating "all the architectural paraphernalia [extra elements] of the Renaissance."[1]

About this time, he changed his name—or at least a significant part of it. He had been christened Frank Lincoln Wright. Like many other boys at the time, he bore the name of the president who saw the country through the Civil War: Abraham Lincoln. Young Wright admired the radical, successful thinkers on his mother's side of the family, the Lloyd Joneses. He adopted the name Lloyd in place of his middle name. He often signed his work F Ll W.

In terms of actual work, Wright had to crawl before he could walk. So the nineteen-year-old Wisconsin native got a job with an architectural firm owned by Joseph Lyman Silsbee. Wright quickly learned that he had one thing in common with Silsbee and most of the firm's other new draftsmen: They were all sons of ministers. Wright worked with Silsbee for several months in 1887, refining and improving his drawing ability. He was paid a starting wage of $8 a week.

Silsbee had prior connections with Wright's mother's family. Silsbee was a member of the Unitarian faith. He had been hired for two projects by Wright's Uncle Jenkin Lloyd Jones, the widely known Unitarian minister. Silsbee designed the Lloyd Jones family chapel near Spring Green, Wisconsin, and the All Souls Unitarian Church for Lloyd Jones's Chicago congregation.

Though Wright said it did not, this family connection probably helped him get a start in the profession he would follow the rest of his life.[2] Wright was able to help supervise construction of his family's chapel and to work on the interior design.

During the period with Silsbee, Frank Lloyd Wright, architect-to-be, read voraciously and greatly improved his drawing skills. About this time, he designed his first building, a private boarding school in Spring Green that would be run by his aunts. The Hillside Home School, as it was known, was coeducational and took in children from all around the valley where Wright had toiled on the farm as a boy. Wright's mother was in charge of the dormitory, and his younger sisters attended the school.

From the beginning, Wright understood how an architect should think: "Conceive the buildings in imagination, not first on paper but in the mind, thoroughly, before touching paper," he wrote. "Let the building, living in imagination, develop gradually . . . before committing it to the drafting board."[3]

In Chicago, the architectural talk of the town was the Chicago Auditorium. It had been designed by "then the only moderns in architecture," as Wright called them: Dankmar Adler and Louis H. Sullivan.[4] Wright presented himself and samples of his work to the firm of Adler & Sullivan late in 1887 and was hired. He was twenty years old at the time.

Adler, older and bushy browed, was the firm's engineer-manager. Sullivan, several years younger and with dark, receding hair, was the artist. During the period of their partnership, the firm of Adler & Sullivan, one of the top firms in Chicago, designed and built more than one hundred buildings. Years later Wright remembered, "They were considered revolutionary and I hungered for revolution."[5] His new job made him feel as if he were "a good pencil in the master's hand."[6]

Wright immediately began to help with the hundreds of drawings needed for construction of the massive Chicago Auditorium building. With ten stories, plus a seventeen-story tower, a huge hotel, and a theater that would become famous for its excellent acoustics, there was an immense amount of detail. Wright and other budding young architects transformed Sullivan's design sketches into working drawings and added a few of their own ideas. It was a wonderful time to be associated with what were becoming very modern building ideas. Sullivan believed that "form follows function," and his architectural designs were organic, inspired by nature.

Wright idolized Sullivan, calling him "*Lieber Meister*" (German for Dear Master). Sullivan gave Wright a number of challenging assignments. While doing such work made Wright a better and better designer, it upset several of the other young employees in the office. Worried because these husky men had begun to pick fights with him, Wright took

Frank Lloyd Wright, age twenty, was hired by a top architectural firm in Chicago.

boxing lessons to learn to defend himself. (Unlike today, in those days boxing was considered a gentlemanly sport.) As it turned out, Wright was in at least two fights with coworkers. Though he won, he was once badly cut up by a foe who had a knife. Clearly, the profession of architecture was not made up entirely of gentlemen.

The group of talented people who worked for Adler & Sullivan became part of what was known as the Chicago School of Architecture. The term referred to the kind of departure from traditional architecture in which Wright and his new friends were engaged. Wright was learning and contributing to the firm. Although he was confident of his enormous talent, Wright was also delighted to find his dream becoming reality. In his autobiography, he wrote about the thrill of seeing the word *Architect* after his name on "a single beautiful clear plate of glass" that was part of the office entrance.[7]

About this time Anna Wright and Wright's younger sister, Maginel, moved to Chicago. Mrs. Wright loved her son dearly and wanted to keep an eye on him. When she discovered that he had a girlfriend, Mrs. Wright was upset.

Frank Lloyd Wright had met Catherine (Kitty) Lee Tobin when he was about twenty and she was sixteen. Despite his lack of experience with women, he was impressive as a suitor. It was a different era, and ambitious young men such as Wright often sought women who would idolize them, raise their children, entertain guests, and never complain.

Although Catherine was from a prosperous family,

when Wright told his mother they wanted to marry, she treated Catherine badly. To her credit, Catherine put up with withering scorn from Anna Wright, who thought that they were too young and that Catherine would never be a worthy mate for her son.[8] And when the young couple walked down the aisle on June 1, 1889, Mrs. Wright drew attention away from the bride and the groom by fainting during the ceremony.[9] It was one week before Frank Lloyd Wright's twenty-second birthday. Catherine was eighteen.

The Wrights started a family quickly after their marriage. To save money, they briefly moved in with his mother and sister Maginel. Maginel felt sorry for Catherine, who was made uncomfortable by Anna Wright.[10] Catherine took to hiding in closets to avoid her mother-in-law.

Fortunately, her new husband came to the rescue. Wright found a plot of land in Oak Park, a Chicago suburb, and proposed to build them a home. The trouble was, he had little or no savings. Catherine's parents did not offer the couple much in the way of a down payment, so Wright borrowed some money from his mother and from Louis Sullivan. From then on, Wright would be a borrower, often living at or above his income level.

Of course Wright designed their new home. It was a wood-frame cottage-style house with a wood-shingle exterior and a generous number of windows. Besides creating a very homey feeling in an inviting living room with a fireplace, Wright included a second-floor studio where he could design buildings away from Adler & Sullivan. He used natural building materials such as brick and wood. The much admired house looked as if it had been carefully put together by a craftsman.

There were solid reasons for having a studio in the home. Wright wanted to design houses, while Adler & Sullivan concentrated on designing larger commercial and industrial buildings. Because Sullivan thought a great deal of Wright, he gave his young friend several houses to design—including a summer home for Sullivan on the Gulf of Mexico in Ocean Springs, Mississippi. Sullivan also handed Wright a couple of assignments designing homes for wealthy Chicagoans.

Wright worked all day long in Chicago and then at night in his home studio. He was lucky the studio was on the second floor, where he could have privacy. In the spring of 1890, Frank Lloyd Wright, Jr., called Lloyd, was born. Then followed John (1892), Catherine (1894), David (1895), Frances (1898), and Robert Llewellyn (1903). The living room was filled with children and with lively goings-on.

Wright constantly changed and added to the house in Oak Park to meet the needs of his growing family. He often rearranged the furniture, changing the look of a room by focusing on different areas. As he came more and more to dislike accessories of any kind, he tossed out nonessentials right and left. He wanted to convince his clients that they should get rid of anything that failed to serve a real need.

Wright had a weakness for aphorisms—sayings that cause the reader to pause and think. He wanted to decorate the inside of his home with many weighty

When Frank Lloyd Wright designed a home for his new bride in Oak Park, Illinois, he paid equal attention to the interior space. Lots of windows and built-in furniture gave the living room a homey feeling.

sayings, but his wife balked. So Wright settled for "Truth Is Life," etched in oak above the fireplace. The more he looked at it, the more Wright wondered if it should be "Life Is Truth."

Wright deeply loved his children, though he worked hard and was often away from home. He provided stylish clothing and music lessons, with each child learning to play a musical instrument. There were many family picnics, parties, and outings. On Sundays, the family attended church. In 1893, Wright added an enormous playroom to his house. The room was the envy of the neighborhood. It had a balcony, where the Wright children gave plays for their friends, and a grand piano. The piano was unusual in that only the keyboard was visible in the room. The rest was suspended by an iron strap and hidden behind a screen wall.

Architectural firms often require their employees to sign contracts promising not to "moonlight." In other words, employees are not allowed to design buildings for their own clients in their spare time. To support his family, Wright needed more money than he was earning. For that reason, he ignored the rule against moonlighting and secretly designed whatever he could. His homes were in demand, and he persuaded a friend to take credit for these designs. In the end this strategy failed, and in 1893, Sullivan dismissed Wright, who had once been his favorite employee.

Now Wright was on his own. The first home he designed in his own practice was constructed in River Forest, Illinois, for William Winslow. The front of the building was simple and graceful, designed in natural colors—creamy brick and white stone, with a dark brown pressed ornamental design on the second story. The house has a broad, overhanging roof. The back of the house, in contrast, was very imaginative with lots of windows, porches, and decks. Shortly after it was completed, a fellow walked into Wright's studio and said, "Now we want you to build our house, but I don't want you to give us anything like that house you did for Winslow. I don't want to go down the back streets to my morning train to avoid being laughed at."[11] Still, many people admired the unusual Winslow house for its simplicity and harmony.

Before Wright left Adler & Sullivan, plans had begun for the World's Columbian Exposition to be held in Chicago in late 1892 and 1893. An important aspect of this world's fair was to be its architecture. Top architectural firms from the United States and Europe were chosen to design the buildings. Designers with a classical architecture style were

Catherine Wright holds the couple's first child, Frank Lloyd Wright, Jr., called Lloyd, who was born in 1890.

selected to design the buildings that would create the exposition's general atmosphere. Adler & Sullivan, whose designs were modern, refused to build in the classical style and had only one building at the fair— the magnificent Transportation Building. Sullivan was aware that the classical style of the other world fair's buildings would influence the architectural thinking of Americans for years to come. He said, "The damage wrought by the World's Fair will last for half a century from its date, if not longer. It has penetrated deep into the constitution of the American mind."[12]

Wright shared Sullivan's deep dislike of the exposition buildings, praising only Sullivan's Transportation Building and the Japanese exhibit. These were strong opinions in view of the fact that the average fairgoer might not even notice the architectural features of the buildings. The constructions were overshadowed by music, amusements, food, games, and various presentations. One newspaper devoted more space to an exhibit of Puerto Rican cigar rolling than it did to the big new buildings. But no one would have been able to convince Frank Lloyd Wright that architecture was not the most important thing at the fair.

Wright was so sure of his feelings that he turned down a tempting offer from Daniel Burnham, president of the American Institute of Architects and the chief organizer of the fair. Burnham had helped found an American academy in Rome for architectural study and was looking for likely young architects to go first to Paris and then to Rome. They would be paid while they studied there. But Wright wanted no part of classical-style architecture, so he turned down the chance to live and work in Europe.

Wright stayed busy perfecting the art of attracting attention. He continued to let his hair grow longer than was the fashion, topping it with a broad-brimmed hat. He often wore an elaborate satin bow tie and a cape and carried a cane. At five feet eight inches, Wright was not a tall man, so dressing in an unusual way helped him to gain attention. Shoes with raised heels also gave him more height.

The only attention he tried to dodge was that of bill collectors. Some even found their way to his Oak Park address. Year by year Wright gained the reputation of delaying payment of what he owed, which was considerable.[13] Several draftsmen worked on and off for Wright in his new studio, built in 1898 and connected to the house by a passageway. Sometimes they were paid; sometimes they were not. In 1893, Wright began to work out of a downtown office as well as his home studio.

Wright by this time had made great strides in his profession and was widely known. Between 1894 and 1911, he created 135 buildings, a large number compared with the work of other architects of his day.[14] After 1910 he also began to produce a steady stream of speeches, articles, and essays. He often expressed strong opinions, such as accusing the American Institute of Architects of being more interested in its members than in its buildings. Always good for a quote, he also believed that throughout the country, "little men were using little brains" to create "confections mistaken for architecture."[15]

The more Wright designed, the more well known and in demand he became. He was gaining a professional reputation not only in the United States but in Europe as well. That reputation was based on Wright's involvement in what would become known as prairie architecture.

Recognition and Scandal

Frank Lloyd Wright was developing a new style of architecture that came to be called the Prairie School of Architecture. Wright believed his true home to be the particular valley belonging to the Lloyd Jones clan near Spring Green, Wisconsin. Surrounded by low hills, and with the Wisconsin River nearby, it was part of the great Midwest prairie. Wright came to see the American prairie, with its tall, waving grasses and few trees, as an especially inviting landscape on which to build a house.[1]

Wright created a home that he felt was ideal for a flat piece of land. The first such prairie house came off his drawing board and was shown in the *Ladies'*

Home Journal in 1901. On the outside it was marked by a low-pitched roof. Everything, in fact, appeared low. He made roofs and ceilings quite low and halls narrow, but other areas within the house were open and wide.

Wright once noted: "It has been said that were I three inches taller (I am five feet eight and a half inches tall), all my houses would have been quite different in proportion. Perhaps."[2] The architect felt that the heart of a building was the space inside it. His design started with the interior needs and worked to the outside. Wright saw architecture as a connection between humans and their environment, and that connection should be as natural as possible. He wanted to shelter people without making them feel caged or confined. He hated the idea of the building as a box with holes for windows and doors, so he created open, free-flowing spaces. Wright shrugged off old and new European designs, believing that they did not apply to the way Americans wanted to live.

His first prairie house also featured overhanging eaves, built-in accessories, a massive central fireplace, windows and porches that blurred the distinction between indoors and outdoors, and a second story that made the building only slightly higher than most single-story homes of the time. Wright called it "A Small House with 'Lots of Room in It.'"[3] He proposed to build several prairie houses on a square block in Oak Park, but the project never began. Then Wright's aunts wanted to enlarge their Hillside Home School in Spring Green, Wisconsin, and asked Wright if he would create a new building. He came up with a pleasing and innovative design.

A number of prairie-style houses went up in the Chicago area, some small but others quite large. Europeans in particular became great admirers of the low-roofed dwellings. Wright's fame increased, resulting in a great deal of work. A typical Wright customer was more interested in having a unique home than in having a more popular-style home. Wright called many of the homes of Chicago's newly rich "fantastic abortions" that were cut up with "box-like compartments." He favored an open floor plan and a connection to the environment.[4]

Wright's homes seemed to grow naturally out of their environment. His was an "organic architecture" that started with the needs of his clients and the natural landscape of the site. Wright resisted building small boxes within boxes and designed spacious, roomy living areas that flowed together, though the bedrooms were often smaller. He used the overhang of the roof to keep the interior shaded in the summer, yet cleverly aimed many windows toward the south for lots of winter light when the sun is low in the sky. To bring in even more light, he placed windows side by side in continuous bands that sometimes turned corners, too.

Wright used the fireplace with a broad hearth as the centerpiece of a house. He ran hot-water heat under window seats for winter comfort and made sure the windows would provide cross breezes to combat summer heat. In streamlining his designs, he minimized basements and excluded attics altogether.

He considered basements "unwholesome," and under a low roof, a living room with a cathedral ceiling simply left no room for an attic.[5] (In the 1930s, when heating technology permitted it, he eliminated the basement, too.)

Modern-day owners of a Frank Lloyd Wright house praise its look, its airiness, and its attention to detail. They may complain, on the other hand, of a leaky roof or impossible kitchen, and few have good things to say about the lack of storage space. Wright paid little attention to the need for closets. He defended his ideas about closets in his speeches and voiced his opinions about the appropriate use of curtains, paint, and other common household items.

Wright's prairie-style houses grew naturally out of their landscape, with low roofs and broad overhanging eaves like this Wright-designed home in Oberlin, Ohio.

Many Wright clients were willing to put up with a few problems in order to have one of his original designs. A number of people came to Wright prepared to do whatever it took to live in one of his prairie houses. One wealthy Chicagoan took to riding all over town with Wright in order to get the architect's opinions before choosing a particular style of house. On one such ride, Wright parked the car at the curb and went inside a new house to chat with the homeowner. He was invited for dinner and recalled three hours later that he had left his customer sitting in the car at the curb.[6]

In 1903, Wright got the opportunity to design an office building, rather than a house. Darwin D. Martin, a businessman who lived in Buffalo, New York, had learned of Wright's architectural abilities through a Chicago relative. He asked Wright to design a headquarters building for the Larkin Company, a growing mail-order firm of which Martin was chief executive. Wright jumped at the chance, despite the fact that he had to put off completing house designs for several Chicago-area residents. He delivered drawings that created widespread interest. The Larkin Building would be particularly American, rather than imitating a classical or foreign style.

The building was made of red brick, loomed six stories above the ground, and introduced a number of features that would be seen in later Wright creations. It was closed off from the outside to keep out noise and fumes from nearby railroad yards. Inside was a rectangular space with an inner open court and tiers of balconies. A vast skylight overlooking the court provided natural lighting. Various offices off the balconies received additional lighting from tall windows. The Larkin Building was one of the first fireproofed buildings and offered central heat. Wright also designed built-in steel office furniture (part of his fireproofing plan) and wall-hung toilets that would make cleaning the floor easier.

The Larkin Building had a great impact on architects at that time. The professional journals praised it as original, though one less enthusiastic critic called it a fortress. European architects, in particular, noted its importance and were influenced by it in designing their own buildings. Wright soon had many new clients.

After years of working day and night, Wright took a vacation in February 1905. He and his wife joined another couple for a trip to Japan. Wright had wanted to travel in the Far East for some time. He had seen Japanese exhibits at world's fairs and was intrigued by the simplicity of design in Japanese houses and works of art. Catherine went with him because she believed being together for a couple of weeks would do their marriage some good.[7]

Wright was impressed with Japanese buildings, and he was fascinated with Japanese art prints. Their simple, uncluttered lines and minimal use of color reinforced what Wright preached—that simplicity was better than complexity, that nature was the ultimate source of inspiration. Wright bought all the prints he could afford, hauling back to the United States hundreds of works of art. For many years afterward he used the prints like money, selling them when he needed cash.[8]

After returning from Japan, Wright was chosen to design a new Unitarian church called Unity Temple and an adjoining recreation building in Oak Park. The old church had been destroyed in a fire. Wright first designed the building in brick, but because the church's budget was quite small, he switched to concrete, one of the oldest and least expensive building materials. Another advantage to concrete was that the construction workers could use the same wooden forms over and over again in casting the concrete. (The forms held the concrete in place while it hardened.)

Wright made the building a work of art. In Unity Temple, he introduced an unusual new style of church architecture. The church was cube-shaped, with massive walls and the appearance of a flat roof. The lighting came from skylights and from windows with geometric designs. Wright said that he wanted the church to be "nobly simple." People were pleased with the completed building, as was Wright. He later wrote, "It serves its purpose well. . . . Its harmonies are bold and striking, but genuine in melody."[9] Unity Temple, completed in 1907, had an important influence on young architects in Europe. In the United States, it was registered in 1971 as a national historic landmark.

Still in his thirties, Wright appeared to be at the peak of his career. The houses he had designed could be seen all over Oak Park and in several other Chicago suburbs as well as in Wisconsin. His reputation continued to grow with the completion of the Larkin Building and as he published additional articles in *Ladies' Home Journal*. He wrote an attention-getting essay called "In the Cause of Architecture" in 1908. Yet Wright was restless, working in bursts that were followed by periods of inactivity.

Catherine fretted over Wright, who became more distant as she became more eager to please.[10] Like her husband, she was an extraordinary, intelligent person. In addition to bearing and raising six children, she was civic-minded, did volunteer work, made speeches, and entertained guests. She and Grace Hemingway, mother of the writer Ernest Hemingway, were important members of a local women's club. Later on, Catherine Wright would become a social worker. But for now she had her own set of problems.

Before Wright completed the Larkin Building, a well-liked and successful engineer named Edwin Cheney had hired him in 1904 to design a house in Oak Park for him and his wife, Mamah. The architect and Mrs. Cheney found themselves attracted to each other. Although Wright stayed extremely busy with his architectural practice over the next several years, their relationship grew. In 1909, Wright asked his wife, Catherine, for a divorce but she refused, still hoping to resolve their marital difficulties.

That year, Wright decided to accept an invitation from Ernst Wasmuth, an important Berlin publisher, to come to Germany to help with the publication of a book about his work—a collection of Wright's drawings, designs, floor plans, and photographs. (It turned out to be one of the most important and famous architectural works ever published and made

Wright met Mamah Cheney in 1904.

a sensation in Europe. Today, single sheets from the Wasmuth Portfolio, as it is known, sell for $2,000.) Wright and Mamah Cheney made plans. They met in New York, and the two of them sailed on an ocean liner for Europe. Their relationship became a public scandal. The *Chicago Tribune* reported that Wright and Cheney were together in Germany. Wright had left his Oak Park architectural practice to two men he hardly knew: Architects Herman von Holst and James Fyfe were offered the business after several of Wright's own employees turned it down.

For part of the year they spent in Europe, Cheney lived in Germany and Wright lived in Fiesole, a suburb of Florence, Italy. She got a teaching job, and he worked with his German publisher while developing new architectural ideas. In October 1910, Wright returned to Oak Park and his family. But Cheney stayed in Europe.

Wright was shunned by friends and neighbors. However, he recruited a wealthy patron, who lent him money to pay his mounting bills. Meanwhile, Wright's mother put her own home in Oak Park up for sale. She bought some land from her brother near Spring Green, Wisconsin, where Wright had worked on his uncle's farm and played as a young boy. There Frank Lloyd Wright would build his dream home, to be called Taliesin. But he had no plans to live there by himself.

Taliesin—and Tragedy

*T*aliesin means "shining brow" in the Welsh language.[1] It was the name of a legendary Welsh bard, or singer-poet. The word had double meaning for Wright, who created his dream home not on the top of a hill but just below it, on the brow, or upper part. Wright designed the Spring Green, Wisconsin, home he called Taliesin to be part of the landscape, so natural it looked as if it had always belonged where it stood. He later wrote, "It was unthinkable to me . . . that any house should be put on that beloved hill. . . . It should be of the hill, belong to it, so hill and house could live together each the happier for the other."[2]

Meanwhile, the Oak Park home was divided into

two parts. Catherine Wright and the children occupied a new home in the studio and part of the house, and the other half was rented out. Wright opened an architectural office in downtown Chicago and lived in an apartment nearby. Sometimes at night Wright would walk past the Oak Park home to be sure the children were all right.[3] Soon he asked his son John to manage his architectural office for him.

There was at least one problem Wright had not counted on. The newspapers learned of the Taliesin building project. Wright's Wisconsin relatives who ran Hillside Home School were dismayed that he was building nearby. Because Wright's reputation was scandalous, his relatives feared that his association with the school might keep parents from enrolling their children. He then issued a public statement that he had no connection with the school.[4] Meanwhile, Wright's pending move to the Spring Green area was the subject of many rumors among its residents. And after her second year in Europe, Mamah Cheney, now divorced, returned to Chicago.

In the fall of 1911, the new home was nearing completion, and Wright and Cheney moved in. On Christmas Day, 1911, he spoke to newspaper reporters at Taliesin to explain and defend his relationship with Cheney.[5] It did little to quiet the rumors or repair the damage to his reputation.

Taliesin, very much a prairie-style house, was more than that. It was a farm, a shop, a studio, a home, a meeting place, a place to entertain, and a refuge from the outside world. Most of this was under one continuous roof. The home would grow and change over many years. Wright always denied being influenced by anyone or anything, but the grounds around the large, low house appeared similar to gardens he had seen in Italy. Soon people began coming to see the strikingly beautiful Taliesin. Over the years it has become one of the most admired houses in the world.

No longer getting many commissions for single-family homes, Wright took on a pair of huge projects and traveled by train back and forth between Chicago and Spring Green to work on them. The first was Midway Gardens. This was a block-square entertainment center on the southern side of Chicago, devoted to concerts, dancing, and dining. Though it has since been demolished, the center was designed to offer Chicagoans a place to picnic and socialize and to let

Wright designed his dream home, called Taliesin, to be a farm, a shop, a studio, a home, and a refuge from the outside world.

them see America's top musicians and actors. Wright's son John worked with him as a construction supervisor on the Midway project. The second project was a proposed $7-million hotel for the city of Tokyo. It is easy to see why Wright wanted the work in Japan: He had long been fascinated with the country's art and architecture.

Though hotel construction did not begin until later, work on the fairyland-like Chicago gardens started immediately. Just as quickly, the project ran into money troubles. Wright's designs were never inexpensive to build, and Midway was no exception. It mixed patterned concrete and brick in the walls and decoration. It had outdoor gardens, stages, and a large orchestra shell. (Wright had learned about acoustics while working with Adler and Sullivan on the Chicago Auditorium.) Artists decorated it with paintings and sculptures. He designed the Summer Garden area for outdoor dancing and dining. The four-story Winter Garden area was enclosed for year-round entertainment. Among the extravagances was a central kitchen with tunnels leading in several directions so that waiters could discreetly hustle food to patrons.

As usual, Wright's own finances were spread thin. He admitted in his autobiography that supporting a family was not the only reason for his constant indebtedness. He spent a great deal of money on luxuries. He dressed in costly and unusual clothes and bought expensive clothing for the children.[6] He also enjoyed owning horses and sporty cars. Wright's major sources of income through the years were

Throughout his life, Wright enjoyed stylish clothes, sporty cars, and horses.

commissions—fees paid by clients for architectural designs—and loans and gifts from wealthy people, whom he often neglected to pay back. He also made money from his books and lecture fees and his profits from selling Japanese art.

Wright had left his family with many bills, in particular a grocery bill of $900. Many years later his son David still remembered that bill with anger.[7] Yet Wright built the costly, isolated Taliesin. Did he build it for himself as a place where he could create dazzling buildings? Did he build it for his mother? Or for Mamah Cheney? Cheney, who was quite well educated, planned to do some writing. His always supportive mother would be there, too, because it was her land on which the dream home was built.

In the summer of 1914, Cheney's two children had come to Taliesin to spend some time with her. A number of workers lived on the site—farmers, farmhands, draftsmen, and carpenters. Wright also employed servants, and on the recommendation of a business associate, he had hired Julian Carlton and his wife, Gertrude. The Carltons were from Barbados. He served as waiter and handyman, and she worked as a cook. Billy Weston, the master carpenter who built Taliesin, described Carlton as polite and intelligent but also as "the most desperate, hot-headed fellow" he had ever met.[8] Tragically, that description would soon become an understatement.

About noon on August 15, Cheney and her children were sitting on a screened-in porch that gave them a view of the Wisconsin River. Inside the house, Julian Carlton served the workers their lunch, then went outdoors. He had hidden several containers of gasoline, which he splashed around the inside and outside of the house. He armed himself with a hatchet and warned his wife to flee before setting Taliesin afire.

The insane Carlton then ran inside the screened-in porch and killed Cheney and her two children. The workers heard nothing. In fact, no one realized anything was wrong until gasoline flowed under the door and flames spread across the dining room. When the workers tried to escape, Carlton attacked them with the hatchet.

He killed four of them. Billy Weston was attacked but not killed. Weston and another injured workman ran to a nearby farmhouse for help, then returned to take up a hose and fight the blaze. Several of the men who survived were badly burned.

Neighbors and the Spring Green Fire Department helped fight the fire, but it was too late. The living area, but not the studio portion, of Taliesin was destroyed in the fire. Before being captured, the deranged Carlton swallowed acid, which badly damaged his mouth and throat. He was taken to the county jail, where he died about two months later. He was never tried, though hearings were held at which evidence was presented.

Frank Lloyd Wright and his son John were at Midway Gardens when Wright received a telephone call telling of the tragedy. John recalled later that his father was so shaken he could barely stand. The two took a taxi to the train station and quickly bought tickets to Spring Green. The Wrights met Mamah

Cheney's former husband, Edwin Cheney, on the station platform. He, too, had received the news of the deaths and was on his way to Spring Green. The two grief-stricken men, Wright and Cheney, silently shook hands.

"She for whom Taliesin had first taken form and her two children—gone," Wright later wrote in his autobiography.[9] The architect was overcome with sorrow over the loss of his love, the attractive, intellectual Mamah Borthwick Cheney.

Soon Wright threw himself into his work in the studio. He was able to forget his troubles only when he was totally busy with creating his designs. While workers cleared away charred rubble and began the process of reconstruction, Wright, now forty-seven years old, spent his days at the drawing board or riding one of the horses from his farm; at night he played his fire-damaged piano or wandered the hills.[10] He broke out in painful boils.[11] In a few weeks he sadly returned to his Chicago studio and apartment. Later, his son John may have summed it up best: "Something in him died with her, something lovable and gentle . . . in my father."[12]

Wright could not ignore the worldwide publicity associated with the murders and the fire. Many in Chicago were quick to condemn him. He was outraged by the criticism. And he was grief-stricken— hundreds of sympathy letters from around the country were tied in a bundle and burned, unread.[13] In Wisconsin, reconstruction was proceeding rapidly. By the end of 1915, Taliesin II was complete.

When Midway Gardens first opened, it was a

popular place. Chicago residents and visitors crowded in to enjoy themselves in a grand setting. But it never lived up to its potential. After World War I began in Europe, the mood of the country became more somber, and many people, cautious about spending money, did not attend places of entertainment as often. In 1916, Midway Gardens was sold to a brewery. It pained Wright to see the site change hands and slowly become an eyesore. The final blow may have been the Prohibition Amendment to the Constitution, which went into effect in January 1920. The amendment attempted to change the drinking habits of Americans by making the sale of alcoholic beverages illegal.

Luckily for Wright, work on Tokyo's new Imperial Hotel began in earnest. After submitting preliminary drawings, Wright was invited to Japan. Since his first visit to Japan in 1905, he had been a serious collector of Japanese prints. Now he was again greatly impressed with Japanese cleanliness, manners, religion, and love of beautiful things.

Wright's Imperial Hotel would become world famous for a most unusual reason. Wright had been warned by the Japanese that their country was subject to earthquakes. His challenge was to create a foundation that would keep the hotel standing during the most violent quake. After much research and many tests of the site, Wright came up with an ingenious solution: He designed the hotel to float on the ground beneath it rather than anchoring it to bedrock. The brick, stone, steel, and reinforced-concrete structure was built on about eight feet of soil on top of as much as seventy feet of soft mud.

Wright's floating foundation, a triumph of engineering, distributed the weight of the big building, but that was only one of several innovations. Wright substituted a handcrafted, lightweight copper roof in place of traditional Japanese tiles. Traditional tiles could be shaken loose by a quake and fall on people running from the building. The hotel was built in sections that would contract and expand when the earth shook. To keep the outer walls from collapsing in an earthquake, he built them wider at the bottom and

Wright wanted to "outwit" earthquakes with his design for the Imperial Hotel in Japan.

thinner near the top. The structure was low, which was usual for him anyway.

Between 1916 and 1922, Wright spent much of his time at the hotel site in Japan, and he was not alone. One of the few sympathy letters he had not thrown out unread after the death of Mamah Cheney was from Miriam Noel. Noel was an American sculptor who had lived in Paris. She had written to Wright as Christmas neared, telling him she understood how lonely the holidays could be after the death of a loved one. A divorced woman, she had departed Paris as World War I fighting intensified, moving to Chicago to be near her married daughter. She told Wright that she had also suffered and thought she might be able to help and comfort him.[14] In his autobiography Wright said, "She was the reverse of everything I had expected."[15] That would turn out to be an understatement about Miriam Noel.

Yet Wright was unable to resist a good story. He grew to enjoy this tall woman with the reddish brown hair who was two years younger than he. She was a member of an upper-class family from Tennessee. Like Wright, Noel loved to write flowery phrases, fashionable at the time. She dazzled Wright by calling him the "Lord of my Waking Dreams!"[16] Unfortunately, unknown to Wright, Noel was addicted to morphine, a potentially deadly painkiller. She also smoked, a habit Wright hated. But eventually Noel moved into the rebuilt Taliesin, as did Wright's mother. And when Wright traveled to Japan in 1916 to supervise construction of the Imperial Hotel, Miriam Noel went, too.

Disappointment in the Twenties

Frank Lloyd Wright was fifty-five years old when he returned to the United States after completion of the Imperial Hotel in 1922. Many countries of the world—including the United States from 1917 to 1918—had been fighting World War I much of the time Wright was in Japan. (He was a lifelong pacifist, disapproving of all wars.) By now, his wife had finally granted him a divorce, his children were grown, and he was thought of as old. Taste in architecture shifted, and Wright's work was less popular. How could that have happened when his designs were still very different from the rows of new houses going up everywhere in the "Roaring Twenties"? Now it was several early-twentieth-century artistic movements in Europe that were grabbing the attention of artists and critics—the people who decide what is fashionable and what is not.

Fashionable movements in the art world embraced new technologies and progress. In architecture, Europeans such as Le Corbusier, Walter Gropius, and Ludwig Mies van der Rohe produced futuristic designs. If Wright's buildings were an organic, natural part of their setting, these new structures were streamlined and boxlike.

Wright got the chance to show what he could do when several wealthy Californians asked him to design houses for them. For inspiration he turned to the original inhabitants of the Americas. He drew on the architecture of the Mayas of Mexico and Central America, building striking residences of concrete blocks. One building surrounded a courtyard garden, a traditional way of coping with a hot climate. Though California smog nowadays is eroding the blocks, these houses show that Wright continued to produce remarkable buildings in the 1920s.

Unfortunately, Wright's personal life was not nearly as successful. After returning to Taliesin, Miriam Noel moved in and out several times, sometimes living in hotel rooms in the Spring Green area. To make matters worse, Noel and Wright's mother did not get along. Wright's mother was at the time battling various illnesses. Soon her health worsened, making it necessary to put her in a nursing home, some seventy miles away. Anna Wright died there, after a few months' stay, in 1923.

Meanwhile, morphine was becoming difficult for

Noel to obtain without a prescription. She suffered severe withdrawal symptoms whenever she was without the drug for more than a day, and her unpredictability tested Wright's temper. Wright was unfamiliar with drugs and believed Noel's illnesses were mental.[1] She saw several doctors, but her problems did not go away. At the urging of his son Lloyd, who had moved to Los Angeles, Wright and Noel went to California. The economy was booming on the West Coast, so if he could not find peace at home, Wright might be able to find it in his work.

A violent earthquake hit Japan on September 1, 1923. At first Wright received news that the Imperial Hotel had been destroyed. He did not believe it. Several days later he received a telegram: "HOTEL STANDS UNDAMAGED AS MONUMENT OF YOUR GENIUS HUNDREDS OF HOMELESS PROVIDED BY PERFECTLY MAINTAINED SERVICE CONGRATULATIONS."[2] Wright's Imperial Hotel was one of only a few buildings in Tokyo to escape major damage. He also learned that the courtyard reflecting pool he had insisted on during construction—for fire protection—had provided the water needed to keep the hotel from burning down. The big hotel remained standing amid the rubble of other buildings.

Writing later, Wright noted that several United States architects had once called the hotel "an insult to American architecture, notifying my clients, and the world generally, that the whole thing would be down in the first quake with horrible loss of life."[3] Wright was proved correct about his design, especially the hotel's floating foundation. As a result, his fame increased throughout the world.

Wright's and Noel's stay in California was not particularly successful, and they soon returned to Taliesin. The couple married in November 1923, but the new Mrs. Wright moved out a few months later. She established a home in California, and Wright actually lost track of her for some time. As in past crises, he immersed himself in creating his designs.

Late in 1924, at a Chicago dance performance by a Russian ballet company, Wright was seated in the same box as a beautiful young woman. He soon struck up a conversation with Olga Ivanovna Lazovich Hinzenberg, called Olgivanna. Then he invited her to a dance after the performance. The white-haired man and the dark-haired woman spun gracefully around the floor to a Strauss waltz. "I fell in love . . . very simple . . . just like that," Olgivanna would later recall.[4] He was fifty-seven. She was twenty-six and had a young daughter, Svetlana. Olgivanna would later become Wright's third wife.

Olgivanna accepted an invitation that Christmas to visit Taliesin, where friends played classical music and she danced in front of the fireplace. She was warmly accepted by Wright's friends. In early 1925, Wright sold his Oak Park home and paid off several overdue debts with his share of the profits. Within a short time Olgivanna came to live at Taliesin.

In April, Taliesin was the scene of a second, very destructive fire. Wright was about to eat his dinner one evening when he noticed that a buzzer in the house would not stop ringing. He attempted to disable

Frank Lloyd Wright shares a quiet moment with his third wife, Olgivanna.

the device and discovered that an electrical short had ignited a fire in one wall. The Spring Green volunteers responded quickly, but the fire, whipped by strong winds, roared out of control. The living quarters were consumed, and the firefighters' goal became saving Wright's studio. Just as all seemed lost, the wind shifted, and a downpour helped subdue the flames. Unfortunately, the home was insured for just $39,000, and total losses amounted to many times that amount.

While in Japan, Wright had collected much art screens, prints, tapestries, antique embroidered silks. A guest from Europe who had earlier visited Taliesin wrote that "there were magnificently painted screens in gold and silver on which were painted either colored flowers or clouds with birds or dark green fir boughs. This estate is like a fairyland."[5] These art treasures located in Taliesin's living quarters were destroyed.

Not even Wright's huge collection of Japanese art prints, which he still had, could bail him out. Market prices were quite low for them at that time. He must have been an optimist, however, for he picked up many pieces from the charred ruins and incorporated them into the rebuilding. Shards of pottery and fragments of stone, marble, and statues went into the newly redesigned Taliesin. Wright soon sent letters to wealthy friends to ask them for loans. To continue his architectural work, he moved his studio back to downtown Chicago.

Complicating Wright's life further was the reappearance of Miriam Noel Wright. Frank Lloyd Wright had filed for a divorce, on the grounds of desertion, in July 1925.[6] His wife asserted that she wanted to save their marriage. Wright made her various offers of money so that she would consent to a divorce, but she refused his offers and began a long, vengeful campaign of harassment. Soon she notified the press that she had been wronged by her husband and filed a succession of legal actions against him.

In December 1925, Olgivanna gave birth to a baby girl, whom they named Iovanna. Wright's lawyer advised against their returning to Taliesin after Iovanna's birth. In addition to Miriam Wright's lawsuits, Wright owed money to a Wisconsin bank, which was threatening to take possession of his fire-damaged home. His lawyer suggested that they go into hiding for some time while he dealt with their legal problems.

Fearing for his safety in dealings with his current wife, Wright, Olgivanna, Iovanna, and Svetlana "disappeared."[7] They spent some time with Olgivanna's relatives and also went to Puerto Rico to help Olgivanna relax and get some rest. During this time the newspapers printed many critical stories about them. Miriam Wright filed charges with the U.S. Department of Justice, claiming that Wright had violated federal law by taking Olgivanna, an unmarried woman, across a state line. Mrs. Wright also charged that Olgivanna, who was not a citizen of the United States, should be deported.

After a few months on the move, Wright and his new family returned briefly to Taliesin. No sooner had they settled into the renovated home than they had a

Wright and his little daughter Iovanna in 1927.

visitor—Miriam Noel Wright. Her lawyer had told her she had a strong claim to Taliesin, and she had decided to take up residence there. She tried unsuccessfully to enter the property several times. Finally, a court official persuaded her to leave after Wright promised to pay her monthly support.

Not long afterward, Miriam Wright filed an "alienation of affections" suit against Olgivanna for $100,000.[8] Wright's lawyers again advised the couple to hide for a while, and they settled into a cottage outside Minneapolis, Minnesota. Warrants for their arrest were issued because of the lawsuit by Miriam Wright and another that was filed by Vlademar Hinzenberg, Olgivanna's former husband. He wanted custody of their daughter, Svetlana, fearing he would no longer be able to see her. Wright was arrested and spent two nights in jail before his lawyers were able to work out the terms of his release.

Hinzenberg dropped the charges when he realized that his daughter was safe. Meanwhile, Wright's financial problems became more severe. Prevented from working, he had been unable to make payments on Taliesin's mortgage. The bank foreclosed. Then a group of friends, fellow architects, former clients, and supporters rallied to Wright's aid. They hired lawyers, worked out plans, invested money in shares, and formed Frank Lloyd Wright, Incorporated. The corporation was arranged to help him pay what he owed and stay out of debt. Wright would work for the corporation, no longer for himself. Later reorganized as Wright, Inc., the corporation negotiated with the bank and was later able to buy Taliesin back for Wright.[9] He sold his precious Japanese prints, but the art gallery that had earlier lent him money on them received the proceeds.

Wright's lawyers continued to negotiate with Miriam Wright for a divorce. She finally accepted a settlement, and the divorce was granted on August 26, 1927. Yet she followed Wright to California. She broke into a home he and Olgivanna had rented while waiting to return to Taliesin.

On August 25, 1928, Wright and Olgivanna were married in California. For more than thirty years, she would be his inspiration, devoted companion, and greatest champion. The couple quietly returned to Taliesin in the early fall.

Wright was enthusiastic about returning to work. Nevertheless, the late 1920s were financially disastrous for him. Lack of commissions forced him to add to his income by writing and giving lectures. He did a series of influential articles for *Architectural Record* magazine, earning a fraction of the amount he routinely had been paid for an architectural project. Though some thought he was past his most productive years, Wright gained a great deal of exposure all across the country by writing sharp criticism and unusual proposals and predictions, paying particular attention to the effects of the automobile on cities. He was an excellent predictor of how cities would expand outward, becoming decentralized.

Wright's name continued to be a familiar one, but the number of new projects declined. He was invited to Arizona to work as a consultant to the architect Albert McArthur on a resort hotel called the Arizona Biltmore. McArthur had seen Wright's concrete block homes on the West Coast and wanted him to create similar blocks for the hotel. Yet shortly after the facility opened, McArthur ran out of money. The hotel was sold to Chicago chewing-gum manufacturer William Wrigley and remains a famous resort to this day.

Wright was asked to design a winter resort in the Arizona mountain desert called San Marcos in the

Desert. To save money on hotel rooms for his family, his apprentices, and his draftsmen, Wright obtained permission to construct several small cabins near the building site. He named this camp Ocatillo. Though the resort project was eventually shelved for lack of funds, Wright developed concepts and techniques for desert buildings at Ocatillo that he would use for the rest of his life.

Other projects were also canceled for lack of money. A Maryland amusement park never got off the drawing board. Designs for an insurance-company skyscraper in Chicago never got past sketches. An apartment tower called St. Mark's in the Bouwerie in New York City was completed only as a small,

The Wright family takes a spin through the Arizona desert in 1929: Frank and Olgivanna, with their little daughter Iovanna (far left), and Olgivanna's daughter Svetlana.

table-sized model. (In 1956, it was redesigned and built as the Price Tower in Bartlesville, Oklahoma—one of Wright's finest designs.) These proposed projects disappeared after the stock market crashed on October 29, 1929, and the Great Depression began. This event marked the end of the building boom in the United States and in much of the rest of the world. Did the economic hard times signal an end to sixty-two-year-old Frank Lloyd Wright's career?

Survival and Rebirth

"**I** have my best work ahead of me."[1] With little or no work, without a savings account, and past sixty years of age, who but Frank Lloyd Wright would have had the nerve to make such a boast? Besides his personal problems, the Great Depression continued throughout the 1930s. Millions of people lost their jobs. Able-bodied adults lined up at soup kitchens because they had no food. When Franklin Delano Roosevelt was elected president of the United States in 1932, he made tough decisions to help the country's economy recover—even closing all the banks for a time. No part of the country was unaffected as wealthy people lost their money and the poor became even poorer. The Great Depression would last for nearly a decade.

Wright always thought of himself not only as supremely creative, but as resourceful, too. Back in 1926, while in hiding in Minnesota, he had begun to work on his autobiography.[2] At Olgivanna Wright's urging, he dictated for long hours to various stenographers. *An Autobiography* by Wright is a poetic blend of feelings and facts. There are wonderful insights, but the author also chose to omit some facts, emphasize others, and embellish some, too. Wright explains in detail why he ended his first marriage. In contrast, Miriam Noel Wright, who caused him so much grief before dying in 1930, receives little attention in the book's pages. Despite Wright's selective details, his autobiography was published in 1932 and sold well. The editors of *The New York Times* thought the book was important enough to justify giving it half a column on March 30, 1932.[3]

Another source of income for Wright was his talks and lectures. In 1930 he was invited by Princeton University to give lectures there on art and architecture. The lectures were very well received, and more invitations from various places followed. Wright was later able to publish the lectures as a book. Another result of the Princeton lectures, known as the Kahn Lectures, was an exhibit of his work, which was sent around the country afterward and led to a European exhibition.

During this time Wright cast repeated glances from Taliesin, still in need of renovation, toward the Hillside Home School, which had been closed for several years. Why not start his own school and use the available buildings at Hillside? Wright contacted

A dapper Frank Lloyd Wright poses beside his Mercedes-Benz.

University of Wisconsin officials to see whether they would be interested in investing money in his school, but they declined. Still, they thought his plans and ideas were promising and urged him to go forward. Like most other corporations in the country, Wright, Inc., was having severe financial troubles. Yet Wright wrote letters to its investors to ask them to support his proposed school. His idea was simple—he wanted to teach young men and women arts and crafts that would allow them to create and sell art. Those arts included ceramics, glassmaking, woodworking, textiles, and metalwork as well as architecture and landscape architecture.

Plans for an applied-arts school did not succeed. Soon Wright had an idea for another school, to be called the Taliesin Fellowship, which was destined to become world famous. In 1932, he sent a group of friends a letter headed "An Extension of the Work in Architecture at Taliesin to Include Apprentices in Residence."[4] The letter announced that seventy apprentices would be accepted to live and work with Wright for a tuition fee of $650 a year. They would study architectural design, building construction, music, and art. They would also do physical work on the farm and maintain the grounds and buildings. They would learn by doing. A relative took one look at Wright's plans and said, "Frank has invented slave labor."[5]

Still, it was a wonderful plan. The Taliesin Fellowship tuition would provide an income for Wright. He would be able to supplement this income with money earned from his writing and lectures. And his apprentices would be learning from a master architect, one of the finest in the world.

At the time, Olgivanna was recovering from tuberculosis, yet she helped Wright get the school up and running. So did the first group of students. They arrived and were put to work doing painting, carpentry, and the many other chores needed to get both the Hillside Home School buildings and Taliesin in working order. The Wrights and their students worked together and ate together, many of the students hanging on Wright's every word. He was an unusual teacher, so to be successful, students had to learn by observing and trying out solutions, not by listening to lectures. In addition to working hard, the students enjoyed parties and picnics, movies and music. Students who broke the rules or did not fit in were often asked to leave or left on their own.

The Taliesin Fellowship does not sound like a radical idea today. But there were few similar co-operative schools in the United States in the 1930s. The students helped raise their own food, built their lodgings, and paid tuition in order to learn to design buildings under the guidance of Frank Lloyd Wright.

Despite the Great Depression, the Fellowship thrived. In the winter, the Wrights and their students migrated west to Scottsdale, Arizona. Among many projects the students helped create was Broadacre City. This twelve-foot by twelve-foot model represented Wright's vision of a community combining the very best of rural and urban life. Wright conceived of Broadacre as a model, not a real plan to be built. It was a guideline for good design of decentralized cities. Such an ideal community as Broadacre had been on Wright's mind for some time. Now, surrounded by talented, high-energy young apprentices, he was able to reproduce it in miniature. The intricately constructed model, which went on display in New York City in 1935, showed his ideas for city planning and attracted much attention.

Broadacre was designed so that every family home would be set on at least an acre of land, to provide space for a vegetable garden. On their land, according to Wright, families would be able to live as they pleased. Apartment dwellers shared a communal garden. Broadacre residents would discover the kind of work they liked to do best and would find markets for the products they developed. There were also businesses, stores, factories, hotels, government buildings, and parks. Wright disliked billboards and telephone poles. He planned for a clean, uncrowded place where "each citizen of the future will have all forms of production, distribution, self-improvement, enjoyment, within a radius of one hundred and fifty miles of his home now easily and speedily available by means of his car or his plane."[6] Wright's ideal Broadacre occupied his mind for years afterward.

Frank Lloyd Wright failed to mellow as he grew older. Elderly Madison, Wisconsin, residents recall him sweeping into a downtown department store, his flowing cape and several of his students following closely behind. He chose expensive clothing for himself, then tried to haggle a lower price from the store owner. Once, on a downtown street, a fellow who believed Wright owed him money punched Wright, breaking his nose. A photo of Wright, sitting in a Madison courtroom wearing a huge bandage, ran in newspapers all across the country.

After the establishment of the Taliesin Fellowship, word of Frank Lloyd Wright's enormous talent was further spread by his students. He was approached by Pittsburgh department store owner Edgar J. Kaufmann, Sr., whose son had enrolled at Taliesin in 1934. Kaufmann wanted Wright to build him a vacation home. He was attracted to Taliesin and thought a similar home would be very appealing in the little glen he owned not far from Pittsburgh at Bear Run, in western Pennsylvania. Kaufmann traveled to Wisconsin and was immediately impressed with Wright. In turn, Wright traveled to the glen, which had a small stream running through it. Wright took a mental picture of the place back with him to his drawing board.

Several stories have sprung up about the design of Kaufmann's Bear Run home, which Wright would call Fallingwater. Wright supposedly thought about the project but did not begin drawing any sketches. One day Kaufmann called Wright from nearby Milwaukee to say he would soon arrive at Taliesin to see the design of his Bear Run home. Wright put down the phone, walked to his drafting room, and began to create what has been called the most memorable private house of the twentieth century. "The design just poured out of him," one student recalled.[7] It is said that Wright finished the sketches just as Kaufmann knocked at the door. This was not unusual for Wright. Ideas would percolate in his mind, and then he would draw them up as if they came out of thin air.

At first, Kaufmann had wanted his woodsy retreat to sit below a little waterfall so that he and his family could look out a window and view it. Wright, taking advantage of the terrain, built the home over the waterfall. He anchored the dwelling in solid rock, enabling him to cantilever, or project, a large structure out over the falls, almost as if it were defying gravity. Kaufmann did not mind at all that he would actually have to step outside to see the falls. Wright had made the building a part of the glen, and the effect was stunning and timeless.

The house was designed to be a natural part of the scenery rather than to look out or down on the cascades of water. There was a great deal of glass, enabling residents to look in three directions from the main floor. Cantilevered terraces projected out over the falls. Each bedroom and a study also had its own terrace. The interior featured a stone floor and stonework on almost every vertical surface, making it seem impossible to tell where the work of nature ended and the work of humans began.

Fallingwater, completed in 1937 in western Pennsylvania, is one of Wright's most famous buildings. "The design just poured out of him," said one of his students.

Besides being the perfect house in the perfect setting, Fallingwater turned out to have the perfect owner. Edgar Kaufmann discovered how to deal effectively with disagreements that arose with Wright. Some revolved around Kaufmann's decision to hire experts to make sure Fallingwater, which seemed to hang in space, was safe. Equally important, Kaufmann was able to afford the cost overruns on the projected price. Even better, from Wright's point of view, Kaufmann wanted other buildings designed for the Pittsburgh area later on.

Wright was as impressed with the completed Fallingwater as everyone else:

> *Fallingwater is a great blessing—one of the great blessings to be experienced here on earth. I think nothing yet ever equaled the coordination, sympathetic expression of the great principle of repose where forest and stream and all the elements of structure are combined so quietly that really you listen not to any noise whatsoever although the music of the stream is there. But you listen to Fallingwater the way you listen to the quiet of the country.*[8]

People through the years have agreed with Wright's evaluation. Kaufmann's son donated the retreat to the Western Pennsylvania Conservancy, and today it is a popular tourist attraction.

Wonderful Work

In 1936, Frank Lloyd Wright designed one of the most brilliant structures of the decade, the S. C. Johnson Wax Administration Building in Racine, Wisconsin. The office building is a curious blend of streamlining and the creative genius of Wright. The company, a prominent manufacturer of floor wax and other products, had already hired an architect for its new headquarters. But president Herbert F. Johnson's associates encouraged him to speak with Wright. After they met, Wright was given the job.[1] During the construction, Johnson and Wright became friends.

The building took three years to construct. One of the main problems was the question of the strength of the internal columns Wright had specified. The thin, reinforced-concrete columns widened greatly at the top and were designed to support the roof and a large skylight. Building inspectors voiced skepticism until Wright actually had a test column built. He then had tons of sandbags and iron stacked on top of it, many times the weight it was required to support. There were no cracks. Satisfied, the inspectors allowed construction to continue.

Like the Larkin Building, the Johnson Wax structure was located in an industrial area. Wright sealed the new building against exterior conditions. The large, airy workroom's ceiling was supported by the slender columns tested earlier. They looked like

Wright's S.C. Johnson Wax building was one of the most brilliant structures of the 1930s.

Inside the S.C. Johnson Wax building, the thin concrete pillars that supported the roof looked like high, round lily pads. Wright also designed the curved-metal desks and chairs.

circular lily pads at the top. Spaces between the columns contained glass tubing, providing natural light for the work areas below.

Wright also designed the furniture for the building, as he often did for private homes. His furniture was always distinctive but not always comfortable. The Johnson building was filled with smart-looking, curved-metal desks and chairs. As for the multistory exterior, it features many curved surfaces of reddish-brown brick trimmed with bands of glass tubing. The effect was so dazzling that the building was featured in *Life* magazine when it was completed. Johnson said, "The building is so beautiful and attractive that I think I'll just put a cot in my office and live here."[2] Wright responded that he would build Johnson a house, and later he did.

Wingspread, as Wright called Johnson's house, was the largest single-family residence Wright built. It had four long, low wings, stretching out in four different directions like a pinwheel. The children's wing had a playroom, bedrooms, and outside swimming pool. There was also a wing for cooking and a pantry, a wing for the parents' bedroom, and a wing for cars and groundskeeping. The living rooms and dining room were at the pinwheel's center. The Johnson family later turned over the spacious residence at Wind Point, Wisconsin, near Lake Michigan to a nonprofit organization for use as a conference center. The wing designed for automobiles was then transformed into offices.

In 1936, the same year he designed the Johnson Wax building, Wright turned his creative energies to a very different type of dwelling. Newspaper reporter Herbert Jacobs and his wife, Katherine, challenged Wright to design a practical, modestly priced house for them in Madison, Wisconsin. To their delight, Wright said, " For twenty years I have been wanting to do a low-cost house, but you are the first people who ever asked me to do one. I have several ideas that I would like to put into a low-cost house, to show America a kind of dwelling that would be much more fit to live in than the crackerboxes that fill the suburbs."[3] Wright's statement was not quite true, as he had already planned two low-cost houses, for clients in Kansas and South Dakota. He had also worked on other low-cost projects throughout his life, including apartments in Chicago and working-class housing in Madison, Wisconsin, and Buffalo, New York.

The Jacobs house was Wright's first Usonian house ever built. *Usonian* was the term he used for his well-designed but affordable housing for middle-income Americans (the residents of USONA—United States of North America). The very appealing Jacobs house was one story, flat-roofed, and built on a concrete foundation containing the steam pipes that provided heating. It was L-shaped, with the living room in one wing and bedrooms in the other. Floor-to-ceiling windows provided natural light. The Jacobs were delighted with their home, and it was built within its budget (just barely). Wright later designed about one hundred Usonian houses, changing the designs over the years. Wright's Usonian plans influenced housing design across the country, especially the modern ranch house.

How many homeowners would be so delighted with their house they would write a book about it? Paul and Jean Hanna did just that after moving into their Frank Lloyd Wright-designed Usonian house in Stanford, California, in November 1937. Their book, filled with color photos, plans, and drawings, tells how their hexagonal "honeycomb" house, on the edge of the Stanford University campus, came to be. It is an absorbing story, not only of a wonderful design but of dealing with its creator.

The Hannas were husband and wife, both teachers and both children of ministers. After reading Wright's published Princeton lectures on modern architecture, they wrote him a complimentary letter. Later, by invitation, the Hannas visited Wright at Taliesin. In 1935, they were ready to build the house of their dreams. They contacted Wright, who seemed to be frequently on the move to or from Arizona. Wright dashed off a set of plans. Despite the fact that the Hannas wanted a single-story home, Wright proposed two stories. Equally puzzling, the plans looked more like a series of geometric patterns than connected rooms. Not a word of explanation accompanied the drawings.[4]

The Hannas purchased a lovely, sloping lot with a southern exposure and hoped for the best. Their requests for changes to the drawings were sent regularly to Wright, but the Hannas could not be sure which changes, if any, he saw or followed. They also told Wright that they could not afford more than $15,000, but he sent them an estimate of $18,000 to build the structure, plus a design fee of $1,800. His disregard of finances was as strong as ever. "Everything gets down to a money matter so quickly," Wright wrote. "Can we avoid it?"[5]

The Hannas asked for a three-dimensional scale model of their dream home, and Wright said he would provide one "next winter"—after construction had begun.[6] That was not soon enough for the Hannas. Using parts from their son's erector set and thin wooden berry boxes, they made their own model. Wright had designed the various rooms in the shape of a hexagon, at 120-degree angles to each other rather than the usual 90 degrees. The rooms flowed into one another with few walls to divide them. "We 'walked' through our model and were surprised to discover the mobility the 120-degree angle gave us," they said. As modest as ever, Wright pronounced the design "about perfect."[7]

The Hannas bubbled over with enthusiasm and sent a steady series of telegrams to Wright, who was in Spring Green. They fired off one message asking for complete specifications and received the following telegram in reply: "OKAY. COMPLYING WITH REQUEST."[8] How, they wondered, could the architect respond to their many letters and telegrams with so little emotion?[9] The Hannas were inexperienced house builders. But Wright, now sixty-nine years of age, had been through the construction process many, many times.

The Hannas had other concerns not directly related to Wright. One neighbor, who was a famed geologist, walked over to the site early in the project and delivered startling information: The Hannas' dream home was being built on a minor geologic fault. (A fault is a break in underground rock along which there is movement, which causes earthquakes.) The Hannas replied that Stanford University had approved the site. The geologist advised them to let Wright know that a branch of the infamous San Andreas fault passed through the very hill on which their house would stand. The Hannas telegraphed this information to Wright. They received the following telegram in reply: "I BUILT THE IMPERIAL HOTEL."[10]

Construction began in January 1937. Jean and Paul Hanna soon learned that Wright's projected budget was wildly optimistic. Before much earth had been moved for the foundation, Wright guessed that the home would cost $25,000. As the Hannas should have expected, Wright congratulated them—and asked for another $1,000 in fees. Muddling matters further, Wright's plans for the foundation of the house were not detailed enough for workers to understand what he really wanted. Meanwhile, in the middle of January, Wright fell ill and was housebound in the middle of Wisconsin, two thousand miles away.

The Hannas' letters and telegrams were usually respectful and fair-minded. But Wright would be clever in one note and the bearer of bad news in the next. On February 2, for example, Wright sent the following telegram: "WISH TO CHANGE LEVELS AND WALLS OF LIVING AND PLAYROOM TERRACES IF NOT TOO FAR ALONG."[11] The Hannas agreed to this and other changes, such as the substituting of materials: for example, concrete for wood. The Stanford University student newspaper called the project "a dream castle," but the Hannas may have thought otherwise at this point.[12]

The Hannas wanted to move into their completed home in September, at the beginning of the school year. In fact they did not move in until late November, and even then the house was not entirely finished. There were wonderful successes during construction, but several errors were made for a number of reasons:

Paul and Jean Hanna were so delighted with their hexagonal "honeycomb" house that they wrote a book all about it.

Wright was sometimes late in supplying details to the construction workers. Because he was unable to be on the site, there was no one to interpret what he meant when he described "organic architecture" (buildings that grow out of their natural surroundings and harmonize with the environment and with their inhabitants). Finally, the building contractor himself freely substituted one material for another when he felt he had a better idea.[13]

In the course of working with Wright, the Hannas learned a great deal about his philosophy of architecture. Houses, said Wright, should conform to the human figure. Wright sometimes took this idea to the extreme, making a passageway to the bedroom of the Hannas' young daughter only twenty inches wide. That made it impossible to move most furniture into the room any way but through a window.

Despite such problems, the Honeycomb House, as it is called, has been judged a wonderful design by virtually everyone who has seen it. (Because of the complex carpentry need for the many angles, the Honeycomb House has not been imitated as the Jacobs House has.) The Hannas raised their children in the house and, in their later years, gave it to Stanford University. It has served as the home of a university official and his family since 1975. This was made possible by the generosity of a major Japanese manufacturer who gave Stanford money to keep the house forever in good repair.

While the Johnson Wax Administration Building, some Usonian houses, and other projects were being built, the Wrights traveled to the Soviet Union. Olgivanna Wright had not been back there since her youth, and the Wrights had received an invitation from the First All-Union Congress of Soviet Architects to attend its meeting in June 1937. Things got off to a bad start when the train carrying the Wrights reached the Soviet border. Everyone on board was required to have customs inspection of baggage, but Wright tucked under his arm several rolls of architectural drawings intended for the meeting and refused to let anyone near them. The resulting tense situation was resolved in Wright's favor, but it was not a good omen.

Wright was received warmly in Moscow at the

architects' meeting. He spoke after a dinner, and his words were carefully translated by his wife. In the speech, he provided details about his architectural philosophy and urged the Soviets to develop their own architecture rather than copy the buildings of other European countries. He also pointed out that the Soviets had a great opportunity to plan their new society. The speech was mild enough, but his mere presence in Moscow attracted the attention of the news media when he returned home.

A number of great designers studied at the Taliesin Fellowship, which would become the Frank Lloyd Wright School of Architecture, headquartered today in Scottsdale, Arizona. In 1937, to house the facility in winter, Wright bought eight hundred acres of rather inexpensive land, then outside Scottsdale. He designed a very different set of structures for his new home and school, which he called Taliesin West. In contrast to the original Taliesin, the Arizona version sits in a valley with mountains in the backdrop. In Wisconsin, visitors gazed out across a valley. In Arizona, they could look out and up, seeing the nearby peaks framed by dramatic slanted wood beams. Those who visited the progressive work-study school were impressed with the buildings, the architectural design, and the young people who helped put them together. Architect Philip Johnson observed that "at Taliesin West, Frank Lloyd Wright made the most intriguingly complex series of turns, twists, low tunnels, surprise views, framed landscapes, that human imagination could achieve."[14]

Now Wright was deeper in debt than ever. One

Wisconsin bank sold the mortgage on Taliesin to a larger bank. That bank threatened to foreclose. Wright was desperate. Wesley Peters, who was married to Olgivanna's daughter Svetlana, put up the money for the mortgage on Taliesin. Peters became Taliesin's new owner.

Afterward Wright began to acquire property surrounding Taliesin. Because of the Great Depression, farmers were desperate in the 1930s, and Wright was able to buy nearby farms cheaply. He ended up purchasing enough land over the next several years to form a large estate, including a stretch of the Wisconsin River's south bank. His students, at least the ones with money, bought other farms nearby. They tore down existing houses or renovated them and created a number of handsome homes for their families.[15]

Fortunately, Wright's fame had increased in the United States and in other countries. In 1932, Wright's work was included in an exhibition of modern architecture at the Museum of Modern Art in New York City. Later, in 1940, the museum would stage a major retrospective of Wright's work, showing his plans and drawings and many photographs of his projects. As more and more people came to know Wright's work, demand for it grew. Despite disagreements throughout the years, the quality of his work had won over most of his critics.

Wright's renewed popularity coincided with one of the darkest moments in world history. Germany invaded Poland in September 1939, and Europe was quickly plunged into war. Any interest in Wright's

On eight hundred acres of land in Scottsdale, Arizona, Wright created a new home and school, which he named Taliesin West.

buildings—Europeans were some of Wright's most loyal admirers—was shoved aside by the conflict. In the United States, rearmament began in earnest. Unemployed persons all over the country found themselves in great demand to work in factories and shipyards as designs for ships and planes and weapons came off drawing boards and were quickly produced.

It surely pained Wright to see hostilities increase between the United States and Germany and Germany's ally Japan. He had long admired Japanese art and life, though the Japan Wright knew in the early part of the century was gone. Militant people ran the Japanese government, resulting in the island nation's invasion of China in 1937 amid a huge military buildup. When the United States entered World War II late in 1941, how much longer could Wright, now seventy-four, continue to turn out highly original work?

Worldwide Renown

By the start of World War II, Frank Lloyd Wright enjoyed a worldwide reputation, both for his stunning buildings and for his strong opinions. People from all walks of life continued to seek him out to design a retail store, funeral parlor, golf club, museum, library, school, church, auditorium, a college campus, and many houses. In 1939, Wright was invited to deliver lectures on architecture in London. And in 1941, King George VI awarded him the Royal Gold Medal for Architecture of the Royal Institute of British Architects.[1]

Americans forgave him his sometimes outrageous outbursts of opinion—or did they? A pacifist, Wright frequently denounced the military draft, condemning

Presidents Franklin Delano Roosevelt and Harry Truman in the process. He seems to have had a blind eye concerning Germany early in the war. He had long held positive opinions about the German people—and German music. Ernst Wasmuth, a German publisher, first published his work and helped him gain an international reputation. Occasionally, Wright voiced unreasoned dislike of England. Even his oldest friends and biggest admirers were outraged. So were some government officials.[2]

The United States resumed the military draft in September 1940. A number of the architectural students at the Taliesin Fellowship registered as pacifists, also known as conscientious objectors. Had they been influenced by Wright to do so? Once the United States entered the war in December 1941, Wright submitted a request to the local draft board asking that these students be exempt so that they could help him keep his farm and architectural business going. The draft board turned down the request. Other Taliesin students joined the armed forces. During the height of the war, there were only a few apprentices left at the Taliesin Fellowship.

Wright spent a part of World War II, beginning in 1943, designing and thinking about a proposed museum in New York City. He may have devoted extra hours to the project because none of his buildings had ever been constructed in America's biggest city. The Solomon R. Guggenheim Museum was the brainchild of a wealthy man who enjoyed modern art and wanted an appropriate building for displaying his outstanding collection.

Wright designed a circular building with an exterior of reinforced concrete spirals. Each spiral juts out more than the one below it, so the building is wider at the top than at the bottom. The main gallery is a continuous spiraling ramp with a gigantic skylight. Visitors take elevators to the top, then walk down the gently sloping ramp to the ground level, viewing the artworks mounted on the walls.

Olgivanna Wright later described the museum's beautiful domed skylight, designed to provide natural light. "The ceiling is a crown webbed in metal and glass through which the light is molded into quiet geometric patterns. From the curved skylights above, the light streams down in soft delicate blue-violet shades as though the sky itself were reflected on the walls."[3] Guggenheim was said to have been greatly pleased by Wright's unusual design, which also takes into consideration that museumgoers do not want to backtrack through a museum.[4]

There were problems from the start with the unusual design. New York City has countless rules for building safety, and Wright had to constantly go over plans for fire exits, rest rooms, and other details. Revisions of blueprints to meet building codes resulted in more delays. Some artists objected to the museum's slanted walls, which would make the top of a painting farther away from the viewer than the bottom. Wright explained that the effect was like viewing the painting on the artist's easel.

Ground was finally broken for the museum in 1956, and it opened in 1959. Despite the delays and the changes forced on Wright, the Solomon R.

Wright was asked by wealthy philanthropist Solomon R. Guggenheim to create a museum for his outstanding collection of modern art. Wright (left), curator Hilla Rebay, and Guggenheim admire a model of the Guggenheim Museum.

Guggenheim Museum is one of the city's premier attractions to this day. Unfortunately, Solomon Guggenheim died in 1949, a decade before anyone visited his monument to modern art. The museum building is itself often praised as being as much a work of art as the treasures housed inside.

At an age when most people think only of the past, Wright—aged seventy-seven in 1944—was obsessed with the future. His energy level was quite high, as he spent long hours at the drawing board, creating more and more imaginative designs. Wright had always been confident of his skills, and advancing age only made him more so. Among his most widely known post-World War II buildings were these:

Herbert Jacobs House No. 2, Middleton, Wisconsin. Wright called this house, designed and built between 1944 and 1948, a "solar hemicycle." Resembling a famous pueblo, the crescent-shaped dwelling was built on a gently rising plot of land, which protected it against the cold of Wisconsin winters. The two story wall of windows was curved to welcome the warm rays of the sun from many angles. Wright also created a roof overhang to shade the windows in the summer. Space was gained for the modest-sized house by suspending a balcony, which contained the bedrooms, from the roof beams, using steel rods.

S. C. Johnson Research Tower, Racine, Wisconsin. Designed in 1944 and completed in 1950, the tower featured floors cantilevered, or projected, from a central "tap root" core that contained stairs, elevator, and utilities. The core extended into the ground. The tower was dazzling. There were no supports at the corners, and, in fact, no square corners. (They were curved.) The tower was constructed of brick, reinforced concrete, and glass tubing and matched the Johnson Wax Administration Building that had been designed by Wright in 1936. Both structures have been designated by the American Institute of Architects as two of seventeen American buildings designed by Wright that should be retained as examples of his architectural contribution to American culture.[5]

Unitarian Church, Shorewood Hills, Madison, Wisconsin. Most small churches in the 1940s were colonial boxes with steeples. Wright drew up plans for the futuristic-looking church in 1947, and it took a couple of years to complete. He said of it, "Unitarians believe in the unity of all things. Well, I tried to build a building here that expressed that overall sense of unity. The plan you see is triangular. The roof is triangular and out of this . . . you got this expression of reverence without recourse to the steeple."[6] The auditorium is also triangular: The plan is based on an elongated diamond shape.

The small congregation, of which he had long been a member, ran out of funds before the church's completion. Wright sent his apprentices to help complete the interior—to paint, plaster, and finish building the furniture. Wright's son-in-law graded the earth for landscaping around the church. Through the years, the congregation and visitors have appreciated the church's truly original, simple design, which has been much copied.

V. C. Morris Gift Shop, San Francisco. Like the Guggenheim Museum, this wonderful store featured a ramp that was the focus of the shop's interior. Unlike the one in the museum, this circular ramp connected only the first and second floors. The shop was a complete remodeling of an older building. Wright designed the solid brick storefront with a bold arched entry of brick and glass. The project was begun in 1948 and was completed in 1950. The artistic design of the building has attracted many shoppers.

Wright's simple triangular design for this futuristic-looking Unitarian church in Madison, Wisconsin, has been much copied.

Mile-High Illinois, a high-rise building, Chicago. Designed in 1956, this daring skyscraper with a television antenna on top would have been four times the height of the Empire State Building. Wright accepted this assignment, despite his earlier criticism of skyscrapers, because he was told that a mile-high television antenna was planned. He believed that a building would be preferable to a huge antenna. His drawings show a building topped by a needlelike structure of incredible height. Wright pictured the building, pressurized like an airplane, as having atomic-powered elevators moving in glass towers. He even planned such details as parking places for cars and landing areas for helicopters. The futuristic project got no further than Wright's busy drawing board.

Marin County Civic Center, San Rafael, California. Wright did not design many buildings for government agencies. This one, designed in 1957, was unusually well thought out. The county board of supervisors wanted a center that could be constructed in segments over a period of years, as tax money became available. The center is located on three low hills with higher hills around it. Across the street sits Wright's only United States government building, the Marin County Post Office, designed the same year. When county officials suggested leveling the hills on the site, Wright said no. He promised to "bridge these hills with graceful arches," and he did so.[7] The center includes the Administration Building, housing county offices, and the Hall of Justice. The center is low, with offices that feature views of nearby hills in one

Wright prepares an architectural drawing for the Mile-High Illinois in 1956. This daring skyscraper never got beyond the design stages.

direction and an enclosed mall in the other. The project almost collapsed when one county supervisor read an untrue statement that called Wright a Communist. Despite the unpleasantness, work on the arched-roof structure started in the late 1950s and was completed in segments over the next ten years.

Wright continued to design other buildings and city plans, one as far away as Baghdad. He also experimented constantly with Taliesin and Taliesin West, changing and rearranging features to match his moods. Olgivanna, who would write several books about her life with Wright, was in charge of day-to-day operations at both Taliesins. She protected him from overeager apprentices, clients, and visitors, shooing away the curious. He took time to write a biography of his old *Lieber Meister*, Louis Sullivan. Happiest when creating designs, Wright had more work awaiting him than at any other time in his life as he approached his ninetieth birthday.

Wright spent much of his last twenty-five years speaking and accepting awards that many believed were long overdue. The American Institute of Architects, a group he had earlier criticized and never joined, honored him with a gold medal. Several universities, including Princeton University (in 1947), Yale University (1954), and the University of Wisconsin (1955), presented him with honorary degrees. He had become one of the most famous architects in the world. In 1956 he even traveled to Wales, the birthplace of his mother's ancestors, to accept an honorary degree from the University of Wales.

Wright did not often show humility, and he seldom praised his assistants. He felt that the humility shown by truly great people was often false. In *A Testament*, his 1957 book, he says that his was great art and that his only influences were his early employers and the world's great poets. "My work is original not only in fact but in spiritual fiber. No practice by any European architect to this day has influenced mine in the least." The Incas, the Mayas, and the Japanese served only to confirm to Wright that he had been on the right track all along.[8] Yet, at

For more than thirty years, Olgivanna Wright was her husband's inspiration, devoted companion, and greatest champion.

one awards ceremony he showed some humility: "I think [this honor] . . . casts a shadow on my native arrogance, and for a moment I feel coming on that disease which is recommended so highly, of humility."[9]

Wright's buildings may have been best judged by one of his clients, the Beth Sholom congregation of Elkins Park, Pennsylvania. Near the end of his life, Wright made drawings for a new synagogue for Beth Sholom and sent them to the rabbi. Awed by the drawings of the building, the rabbi wrote, "You have taken the supreme moment of Jewish history—the revelation of God to Israel through Moses at Mount Sinai, and you have translated that moment with all it signifies into a design of beauty and reverence."[10] Such was the impact of a building designed by Frank Lloyd Wright.

Frank Lloyd Wright's Legacy

By the spring of 1959, Frank Lloyd Wright appeared to be feeling the weight of his ninety-one years. He enjoyed the elaborate annual Easter celebration at Taliesin West in late March with several members of his family, students, and many guests. A few days later, complaining of stomach pains, he was admitted to a Phoenix hospital. Wright survived an operation to remove a blockage from his intestine. But two days later, on the evening of April 9, 1959, a nurse heard him sigh, and in a few moments he was dead.

The following day, a son-in-law who had studied under him and an apprentice loaded the coffin containing the body of Frank Lloyd Wright into the back of a pickup truck. They drove nonstop to Wisconsin. A Unitarian service was held in the living room at Taliesin on April 12. The coffin was then placed on a small farm wagon, covered with pine boughs and flowers, and pulled to the family burial ground by two sturdy horses. A number of family members, friends, and acquaintances followed the wagon on foot to the grave, just down the hill from Taliesin. Frank Lloyd Wright's tombstone would read, "Love of an idea is love of God."[1] It was just a few months before the splendid Guggenheim Museum would open.

The stone remains. But after Olgivanna Wright's death in 1985, as she had instructed, Wright's body was taken up, cremated, and placed near hers in a niche in a garden wall at Taliesin West.[2]

Wright was remarkable in many ways, not the least of which is that he was productive for more than seventy years. He revolutionized the way many Americans look at buildings, houses in particular. He constantly experimented and created many innovations that are now commonplace construction practices. He was also the author of many books, including *An Autobiography*, *A Testament*, *An Organic Architecture*, and *The Natural House*. He wrote dozens of architectural articles and many speeches. His career stretched from 1886, when most Civil War veterans were still living, to 1959, when Dwight Eisenhower was president, a period of incredible change. Yet even his century-old designs remain fresh to the eye today.

The Frank Lloyd Wright Archives hold more than twenty-one thousand of his plans, sketches,

Frank Lloyd Wright's career spanned three fourths of a century, and even his century-old designs remain fresh to the eye today.

renderings, and working drawings.[3] About five hundred of his works were built, and about one hundred have been destroyed.[4] A majority of his buildings were single-family houses. Not all of the designs were great, of course, and several of the great structures have been torn down. They include Chicago's Midway Gardens, leveled in 1929; the Larkin Building in Buffalo, New York, demolished in 1950; the original Hillside Home School in Spring Green, Wisconsin, torn down in 1950; and the Imperial Hotel in Tokyo. The hotel survived earthquakes and World War II, only to be knocked down to make way for a high-rise hotel in 1967.

Yet Wright's fame continues in the years since his death. It is safe to say that Frank Lloyd Wright may be the only architect, past or present, whose name is known to the average American. It is also a good bet that every Wright-designed building still standing (there are Wright-designed buildings in thirty-six states) will not be torn down but will be maintained endlessly as a salute to great design and to the world-renowned architect.

The Frank Lloyd Wright Foundation now allows the reproduction of his designs. Patterns and designs from his work have been copied onto fabrics, wall coverings, calendars, china, silver, glass, and more. The Museum of Modern Art sells a number of items, from a cherrywood barrel chair designed in 1904 to a slim wooden desk created in 1908. Some of the money goes to the Wright Foundation.

The foundation also produces a magazine,

Quarterly, devoted to Wright's life and work. The World Wide Web contains numerous sites devoted to Frank Lloyd Wright, covering everything from his best quotations to details on his buildings.

In the early 1990s, a dramatic salute to Wright took place in what many consider his hometown. Madison, Wisconsin, dusted off a design by Wright of a civic center for the city. Created for the shore of Lake Monona on the southeastern edge of Madison's downtown, Monona Terrace was designed by Wright in 1938. It was completed in 1007, a gap of fifty-nine years. The modern-looking center appears remarkably like Wright's original plans, though new construction techniques and technology have made for slight differences. The huge, cream-colored

Wright's 1938 design for the Monona Terrace civic center (the curved building complex along the waterfront in this picture) was revived and built more than thirty years after Wright's death.

structure houses conventions and other large meetings. Officially, the center is known as the Frank Lloyd Wright Lake Monona Community and Convention Center.

Who knows how many more Wright designs will be transformed from pencil and paper to bricks, stone, steel, and glass? In a very real sense, Frank Lloyd Wright and his ideas continue to live through his work.

Chronology

1867—Frank Lloyd Wright is born on June 8 in Richland Center, Wisconsin.

1869—The Wright family makes the first of several moves around the country in search of financial opportunity.

1878—The family returns to Wisconsin, moving to Madison.

1885—Frank's parents, William Russell Cary Wright and Anna Lloyd Jones Wright, are divorced.

1886—Frank Lloyd Wright spends one year at the University of Wisconsin as a student of civil engineering.

1887—Takes a job with an architectural firm in Chicago.

1889—Marries Catherine Lee Tobin, who will bear him six children.

1893—Leaves the architectural firm Adler & Sullivan and opens an office to work on his own designs, mostly private residences.

1894—First exhibit of Wright's work held at the Chicago Architectural Club.

1901—Perfects the long, low look of the prairie-style home in several projects.

1905—Makes his first trip to Japan.

1909—Leaves his architectural practice and his family to go with Mamah Cheney on his first trip to Europe, where his professional reputation is growing.

1910—A German company publishes an edition of Wright's work, known as the *Wasmuth Portfolio*.

1911—Travels again to Berlin; returns to build Taliesin, his home and studio, near Spring Green, Wisconsin.

1913—Returns to Japan, seeking the commission for designing and building the Imperial Hotel in Tokyo.

1914—A deranged servant murders Mamah Cheney and six others and burns Taliesin.

1916—Sails to Japan with Miriam Noel to work on the Imperial Hotel.

1922—Divorce from Catherine is finalized; Wright opens an office in Los Angeles.

1923—Wright's mother, to whom he was devoted, dies; he marries Miriam Noel.

1923—Working with his son Lloyd, builds concrete-
–1924 block houses in California.

1924—Separates from Miriam Noel Wright; meets Olgivanna Lazovich Hinzenberg.

1925—Taliesin burns for the second time, destroying the living quarters.

1927—Begins a series of monthly articles called "In the Cause of Architecture" in *The Architectural Record*; is divorced from Miriam Noel.

1928—Olgivanna Hinzenberg becomes his third wife.

1930—Lectures at Princeton University.

1932—Founds the Taliesin Fellowship, which would become the Frank Lloyd Wright School of Architecture; publishes *An Autobiography* and *The Disappearing City*, his prediction of the modern decentralized city; his work is shown in New York at the Museum of Modern Art's exhibition of modern architecture.

1935—Pennsylvania department-store owner Edgar J. Kaufmann commissions Wright to design the architect's most famous private residence, Fallingwater, under construction 1936–1937; displays a model of Broadacre City in New York and then around the country.

1936—Builds the first of his Usonian houses, for Herbert Jacobs.

1937—Travels to the Soviet Union to attend the First All-Union Congress of Soviet Architects; begins to build Taliesin West in Scottsdale, Arizona, as a winter home and winter quarters for the Taliesin Fellowship.

1939—Delivers a series of lectures in London on organic architecture.

1940—A major retrospective exhibition of Wright's work is held at the Museum of Modern Art; Wright founds the Frank Lloyd Wright Foundation.

1941—Awarded the Royal Gold Medal for Architecture by the Royal Institute of British Architects.

1943—Publishes his revised and enlarged autobiography; Solomon R. Guggenheim commissions Wright to design a museum, which is not finished until 1959.

1949—Publishes a biography of Louis Sullivan; awarded the Gold Medal of the American Institute of Architects.

1951—The "Sixty Years of Living Architecture" exhibition of Wright's designs, including models, photographs, and drawings, begins a world tour in Florence, Italy, and is a hit.

1957—Designs the Marin County Civic Center; flies to Baghdad and is commissioned by the king of Iraq to design a complex of buildings featuring an opera house (never built after the king's death).

1959—Begins work on a book for teenagers called *The Wonderful World of Architecture*; dies in Phoenix, Arizona, on April 9 at the age of ninety-one.

Buildings by Frank Lloyd Wright

A Selected List

Frank Lloyd Wright Home and Studio, Oak Park, Illinois (1889)

Larkin Company Administration Building, Buffalo, New York (1903, demolished 1950)

Unity Temple, Oak Park, Illinois (1905)

Frederick C. Robie House, Chicago, Illinois (1906)

Taliesin I, Spring Green, Wisconsin (1911)

Midway Gardens, Chicago, Illinois (1913, demolished 1929)

Imperial Hotel, Tokyo, Japan (1915–1922, demolished 1967)

Aline Barnsdall House, "Hollyhock House," Los Angeles, California (1917)

John Storer House, Hollywood, California (1923)

Jean S. and Paul R. Hanna House, "Honeycomb House," Stanford, California, (1935–1937)

Edgar J. Kaufmann House, "Fallingwater," Bear Run, Pennsylvania (1935)

Herbert Jacobs House I, Usonian house, Madison, Wisconsin (1936)

S. C. Johnson Wax building complex, Racine, Wisconsin (1936–1939, 1944–1950)

Herbert F. Johnson House, "Wingspread," Racine, Wisconsin (1937)

Taliesin West, Scottsdale, Arizona (1937)

Goetsch-Winckler House, Okemos, Michigan (1939)

Solomon R. Guggenheim Museum, New York, New York (1943–1959)

Herbert Jacobs House II, "The Solar Hemicycle," Middleton, Wisconsin (1944–1948)

V. C. Morris Gift Shop, San Francisco, California (1948)

H. C. Price Company Tower, Bartlesville, Oklahoma (1952)

Beth Sholom Synagogue, Elkins Park, Pennsylvania (1954)

Kalita Humphreys Theater, Dallas Texas (1955)

Marin County Civic Center, San Rafael, California (1957)

Chapter Notes

Chapter 1. Witness to Tragedy

1. *Wisconsin State Journal* (Madison), November 9, 1883 (clipping courtesy of the State Historical Society of Wisconsin, Madison, Wisconsin).

2. Olgivanna Lloyd Wright, *Frank Lloyd Wright: His Life, His Work, His Words* (New York: Horizon Press, 1966), p. 19.

3. Ibid., p. 18.

4. Frank Lloyd Wright, *An Autobiography* (New York. Horizon Press, 1943, 1977), p. 70.

5. Ibid.

6. Olgivanna Lloyd Wright, pp. 19–20.

7. Frank Lloyd Wright, p. 76.

Chapter 2. "A Prophetic Birth"

1. Meryle Secrest, *Frank Lloyd Wright* (New York: Knopf, 1992), pp. 52–53.

2. Olgivanna Lloyd Wright, *Frank Lloyd Wright: His Life, His Work, His Words* (New York: Horizon Press, 1966), p. 11.

3. Secrest, pp. 68–69.

4. Ibid., p. 66.

5. Frank Lloyd Wright, *An Autobiography* (New York: Horizon Press, 1943, 1977), p. 33.

6. Herbert Jacobs, *Frank Lloyd Wright: America's Greatest Architect* (New York: Harcourt, Brace & World, 1965), p. 23.

7. Edgar Kaufmann and Ben Raeburn, eds., *Frank Lloyd Wright: Writings and Buildings* (New York: New American Library, 1960), p. 19.

8. Frank Lloyd Wright, p. 38.

9. Ibid.

10. Ibid., p. 40.

11. Ibid.

12. Jacobs, p. 21.

13. Secrest, p. 63.

14. Frank Lloyd Wright, p. 55.

15. Ibid., p. 58.

16. Ibid., p. 77.

Chapter 3. The Dawn of Change

1. Edgar Kaufmann and Ben Raeburn, eds., *Frank Lloyd Wright: Writings and Buildings* (New York: New American Library, 1960), p. 21.

2. Brendan Gill, *Many Masks: A Life of Frank Lloyd Wright* (New York: Putnam, 1987), pp. 57–58.

3. Kaufmann and Raeburn, p. 221.

4. Ibid., p. 21.

5. Patrick J. Meehan, ed., *The Master Architect: Conversations with Frank Lloyd Wright* (New York: Wiley, 1984), p. 12.

6. Ibid.

7. Frank Lloyd Wright, *An Autobiography* (New York: Horizon Press, 1943, 1977), p. 149.

8. Meryle Secrest, *Frank Lloyd Wright* (New York: Knopf, 1992), p. 102.

9. Ibid.

10. Ibid., p. 111.

11. Bruce Brooks Pfeiffer, *Frank Lloyd Wright: The Masterworks* (New York: Rizzoli, 1993), p. 26.

12. Finis Farr, *Frank Lloyd Wright: A Biography* (New York: Scribner, 1961), p. 51.

13. Gill, p. 102.

14. Secrest, p. 161.

15. Kaufmann and Raeburn, p. 33.

Chapter 4. Recognition and Scandal

1. Edgar Kaufmann and Ben Raeburn, eds., *Frank Lloyd Wright: Writings and Buildings* (New York: New American Library, 1960), p. 38.

2. Ibid., p. 42.

3. Robert C. Twombly, *Frank Lloyd Wright: An Interpretive Biography* (New York: Harper & Row, 1973), pp. 48–49.

4. Ibid., p. 53.

5. Meryle Secrest, *Frank Lloyd Wright* (New York: Knopf, 1992), p. 170.

6. Ibid., p. 172.

7. Ibid., p. 185.

8. Ibid., p. 187.

9. Kaufmann and Raeburn, p. 82.

10. Brendan Gill, *Many Masks: A Life of Frank Lloyd Wright* (New York: Putnam, 1987), pp. 201–202.

Chapter 5. Taliesin—and Tragedy

1. Edgar Kaufmann and Ben Raeburn, eds., *Frank Lloyd Wright: Writings and Buildings* (New York: New American Library, 1960), p. 172.

2. Ibid., p. 173.

3. Herbert Jacobs, *Frank Lloyd Wright: America's Greatest Architect* (New York: Harcourt, Brace & World, 1965), pp. 76–77.

4. Brendan Gill, *Many Masks: A Life of Frank Lloyd Wright* (New York: Putnam, 1987), p. 216.

5. Ibid., p. 221.

6. Frank Lloyd Wright, *An Autobiography* (New York: Horizon Press, 1943, 1977), p. 140.

7. Meryle Secrest, *Frank Lloyd Wright* (New York: Knopf, 1992), p. 204.

8. Ibid., p. 217.

9. Wright, p. 209

10. Jacobs, p. 87.

11. Secrest, p. 222.

12. Robert C. Twombly, *Frank Lloyd Wright: An Interpretive Biography* (New York: Harper & Row, 1973), p. 138.

13. Finis Farr, *Frank Lloyd Wright: A Biography* (New York: Scribner, 1961), p. 146.

14. Ibid., p. 147.

15. Wright, pp. 224–225.

16. Secrest, p. 241.

Chapter 6. Disappointment in the Twenties

1. Brendan Gill, *Many Masks: A Life of Frank Lloyd Wright* (New York: Putnam, 1987), p. 287.

2. Alexander O. Boulton, *Frank Lloyd Wright: Architect* (New York: Rizzoli, 1993), p. 68.

3. Edgar Kaufmann and Ben Raeburn, eds., *Frank Lloyd Wright: Writings and Buildings* (New York: New American Library, 1960), p. 207.

4. Meryle Secrest, *Frank Lloyd Wright* (New York: Knopf, 1992), p. 312.

5. Kathryn Smith, *Frank Lloyd Wright's Taliesin and Taliesin West* (New York: Harry N. Abrams, 1997), p. 50.

6. Secrest, pp. 314–315.

7. Ibid., p. 324.

8. Gill, p. 294.

9. Secrest, p. 342.

Chapter 7. Survival and Rebirth

1. Brendan Gill, *Many Masks: A Life of Frank Lloyd Wright* (New York: Putnam, 1987), p. 321.

2. Alexander O. Boulton, *Frank Lloyd Wright: Architect* (New York: Rizzoli, 1993), p. 74.

3. Meryle Secrest, *Frank Lloyd Wright* (New York: Putnam, 1992), p. 385.

4. Gill, p. 328.

5. Secrest, p. 399

6. Gill, p. 337.

7. Ibid., p. 346.

8. Bruce Brooks Pfeiffer, *Frank Lloyd Wright: The Masterworks* (New York: Rizzoli, 1993), p. 161.

Chapter 8. Wonderful Work

1. Bruce Brooks Pfeiffer, *Frank Lloyd Wright: The Masterworks* (New York: Rizzoli, 1993), p. 176.

2. Herbert Jacobs, *Frank Lloyd Wright: America's Greatest Architect* (New York: Harcourt, Brace & World, 1965), p. 126.

3. Ibid., p. 128.

4. Paul R. Hanna and Jean S. Hanna, *Frank Lloyd Wright's Hanna House: The Clients' Report* (New York: Architectural History Foundation/MIT Press, 1981), p. 19.

5. Ibid., p. 24.

6. Ibid., p. 28.

7. Ibid.

8. Ibid., p. 31.

9. Ibid.

10. Ibid.

11. Ibid., p. 54.

12. Ibid., p. 57.

13. Ibid., p. 76.

14. Kathryn Smith, *Frank Lloyd Wright's Taliesin and Taliesin West* (New York: Harry N. Abrams, 1997), p. 90.

15. Meryle Secrest, *Frank Lloyd Wright* (New York: Knopf, 1992), p. 439.

Chapter 9. Worldwide Renown

1. Brendan Gill, *Many Masks: A Life of Frank Lloyd Wright* (New York: Putnam, 1987), p. 405.

2. Ibid.

3. Olgivanna Lloyd Wright, *Frank Lloyd Wright: His Life, His Work, His Words* (New York: Horizon Press, 1966), pp. 164–165.

4. Bruce Brooks Pfeiffer, *Frank Lloyd Wright: The Masterworks* (New York: Rizzoli, 1993), p. 209.

5. William Allin Storrer, *The Frank Lloyd Wright Companion* (Chicago: University of Chicago Press, 1993), p. 248.

6. Pfeiffer, p. 227.

7. Ibid., p. 273.

8. Edgar Kaufmann and Ben Raeburn, eds., *Frank Lloyd Wright: Writings and Buildings* (New York: New American Library, 1960), p. 301.

9. Meryle Secrest, *Frank Lloyd Wright* (New York: Knopf, 1992), p. 522.

10. Pfeiffer, p. 264.

Chapter 10. Frank Lloyd Wright's Legacy

1. Brendan Gill, *Many Masks: A Life of Frank Lloyd Wright* (New York: Putnam, 1987), p. 501.

2. Alexander O. Boulton, *Frank Lloyd Wright: Architect* (New York: Rizzoli, 1993), p. 105.

3. Bruce Brooks Pfeiffer, *Frank Lloyd Wright: The Masterworks* (New York: Rizzoli, 1993), p. 309.

4. William Allin Storrer, *The Frank Lloyd Wright Companion* (Chicago: University of Chicago Press, 1993), p. xi.

Further Reading

Boulton, Alexander O. *Frank Lloyd Wright: Architect.* New York: Rizzoli, 1993.

Davis, Francis A. *Frank Lloyd Wright: Maverick Architect.* Minneapolis: Lerner, 1996.

Hanna, Paul R., and Jean S. Hanna. *Frank Lloyd Wright's Hanna House: The Clients' Report.* New York: The Architectural History Foundation/MIT Press, 1981.

Jacobs, Herbert. *Frank Lloyd Wright: America's Greatest Architect.* New York: Harcourt, Brace & World, 1965.

Kaufmann, Edgar, and Ben Raeburn, eds. *Frank Lloyd Wright: Writings and Buildings.* New York: New American Library, 1960.

Lind, Carla. *Lost Wright: Frank Lloyd Wright's Vanished Masterpieces.* New York: Simon & Schuster, 1996.

McDonough, Yona Zeldis. *Frank Lloyd Wright.* New York: Chelsea House, 1992.

Murphy, Wendy Buehr. *Frank Lloyd Wright—Genius!: The Artist and the Process.* Englewood Cliffs, N.J.: Silver Burdett Press, 1990.

Pfeiffer, Bruce Brooks. *Frank Lloyd Wright: The Masterworks.* New York: Rizzoli, 1993.

Rubin, Susan Goldman. *Frank Lloyd Wright.* New York: Harry N. Abrams, 1994.

Thorne-Thomsen, Kathleen. *Frank Lloyd Wright for Kids.* Chicago: Chicago Review Press, 1994.

Wright, Frank Lloyd. *An Autobiography.* New York: Horizon Press, 1943, 1977.

Wright, Olgivanna Lloyd. *Our House.* New York: Horizon Press, 1959.

———. *The Shining Brow: Frank Lloyd Wright.* New York: Horizon Press, 1960.

———. *Frank Lloyd Wright: His Life, His Work, His Words.* New York: Horizon Press, 1966.

• • • •

The Frank Lloyd Wright Foundation. *Taliesin West,* Scottsdale, Arizona 85261. (602) 860-2700.

Internet Addresses

Frank Lloyd Wright Source Page

<http://www.mcs.com/~tgiesler/flw_home.htm>

The Frank Lloyd Wright Foundation

<http://www.franklloydwright.org>

Frank Lloyd Wright Appreciation Page

<http://members.aol.com/ddukesf/index.html>

Wright at Home

<http://www.erols.com/dchandlr/fllw.htm>

Frank Lloyd Wright in Oak Park, Illinois, 1889–1909

<http://www.oprf.com/flw/welcome.html>

All-Wright Site

<http://www.geocities.com/SoHo/1469/flw.html>

Index

1/08